M
WORK OUT
SERIES

Work Out

Accounting

GCSE

The titles in this series

MACMILLAN
WORK OUT
SERIES

Work Out

Accounting

GCSE

P. Stevens

MACMILLAN

To Darren and Dawn

First published in 1986 by
THE MACMILLAN PRESS LTD
Houndmills, Basingstoke, Hampshire RG21 2XS
and London
Companies and representatives
throughout the world

ISBN 0–333–44012–9
ISBN 0–333–43455–2 Export

A catalogue record for this book
is available from the British Library.

Printed and bound by Unwin Brothers Ltd.,
The Gresham Press, Old Woking, Surrey GU22 9LH
A Member of the Martins Printing Group

First edition (with corrections) reprinted twice
Second edition 1987
10   9   8   7   6   5
00   99   98   97   96   95   94   93   92

Contents

Acknowledgements

The University of London Entrance and School Examinations Council accepts no responsibility whatsoever for the accuracy or method in the answers given in this book to actual questions set by the London Board.

Acknowledgement is made to the Southern Universities' Joint Board for School Examinations for permission to use questions taken from their past papers but the Board is in no way responsible for answers that may be provided and they are solely the responsibility of the authors.

The Associated Examining Board, the University of Oxford Delegacy of Local Examinations, and the Scottish Examination Board wish to point out that worked examples included in the text are entirely the responsibility of the author and have neither been provided nor approved by the Board.

The author and publishers wish to thank the following who have kindly given permission for the use of copyright material: The Associated Examining Board, The Scottish Examination Board, the Southern Universities' Joint Board, The University of London School Examinations Board, The University of Oxford Delegacy of Local Examinations for questions from past examination papers.

Every effort has been made to trace all the copyright holders, but if any have been inadvertently overlooked, the publishers will be pleased to make the necessary arrangement at the first opportunity.

Organisations Responsible for GCSE Examinations

In the United Kingdom, examinations are administered by the following organisations. Syllabuses and examination papers can be ordered from the addresses given here:

Northern Examining Association (NEA)

Joint Matriculation Board (JMB)
Publications available from:
John Sherratt & Son Ltd
78 Park Road, Altrincham
Cheshire WA14 5QQ

North Regional Examinations Board
Wheatfield Road, Westerhope
Newcastle upon Tyne NE5 5JZ

Yorkshire and Humberside Regional Examinations Board (YREB)
Scarsdale House
136 Derbyside Lane
Sheffield S8 8SE

Associated Lancashire Schools Examining Board
12 Harter Street
Manchester M1 6HL

North West Regional Examinations Board (NWREB)
Orbit House, Albert Street
Eccles, Manchester M30 0WL

Midland Examining Group (MEG)

**University of Cambridge Local
Examinations Syndicate (UCLES)**
Syndicate Buildings, Hills Road
Cambridge CB1 2EU

**Oxford and Cambridge Schools
Examination Board (O & C)**
10 Trumpington Street
Cambridge CB2 1QB

Southern Universities' Joint Board (SUJB)
Cotham Road
Bristol BS6 6DD

**East Midland Regional Examinations
Board (EMREB)**
Robins Wood House, Robins Wood Road
Aspley, Nottingham NG8 3NR

**West Midlands Examinations Board
(WMEB)**
Norfolk House, Smallbrook
Queensway, Birmingham B5 4NJ

London and East Anglian Group (LEAG)

**University of London School
Examinations Board (L)**
University of London Publications Office
52 Gordon Square
London WC1E 6EE

**London Regional Examining Board
(LREB)**
Lyon House
104 Wandsworth High Street
London SW18 4LF

East Anglian Examinations Board (EAEB)
The Lindens, Lexden Road
Colchester, Essex CO3 3RL

Southern Examining Group (SEG)

The Associated Examining Board (AEB)
Stag Hill House
Guildford, Surrey GU2 5XJ

**University of Oxford Delegacy of
Local Examinations (OLE)**
Ewert Place, Banbury Road
Summertown, Oxford OX2 7BZ

**Southern Regional Examinations
Board (SREB)**
Avondale House, 33 Carlton Crescent
Southampton, Hants SO9 4YL

**South-East Regional Examinations
Board (SEREB)**
Beloe House, 2–10 Mount Ephraim Road
Royal Tunbridge Wells, Kent TN1 1EU

**South-Western Examinations
Board (SWExB)**
23–29 Marsh Street
Bristol BS1 4BP

Scottish Examination Board (SEB)

Publications available from:
Robert Gibson and Sons (Glasgow) Ltd
17 Fitzroy Place, Glasgow G3 7SF

Welsh Joint Education Committee (WJEC)

245 Western Avenue
Cardiff CF5 2YX

Northern Ireland Schools Examinations Council (NISEC)

Examinations Office
Beechill House, Beechill Road
Belfast BT8 4RS

Introduction

How to Use this Book

This book is primarily intended for students who have already studied some book-keeping. However, since all the principles and techniques are illustrated in the relevant chapters, it is not a prerequisite to have any previous knowledge.

You are recommended to read a chapter, understanding each technique which is being explained, before proceeding to the next point. You should then study the worked examples and solutions, making sure that you fully understand how the solutions have been arrived at, and why.

Only when you are sure you have completed this stage should you proceed to the Further Exercises. These should be attempted without reference to the answers that follow; use the answers given to compare with your own, to ensure that you have fully understood the subject matter.

The book contains over 100 questions from past papers set by various examination bodies, and if you successfully work through these, you will be adequately prepared to achieve success in your examination.

Revision

Before you start to revise, find out exactly which syllabus you are following and obtain a copy of it. The book contains many questions from the most recent examination papers of various examination boards. However, having worked through these, you may wish to obtain copies of past papers from your own examination board. Certainly the best way to check your revision progress in Accounting is to work carefully through as many typical questions as you possibly can. Take a topic at a time, make certain that you understand fully the key points of theory and then attempt a range of questions.

The examination

In practical accounting examinations it is vital that you allocate the time you spend on each question according to the number of marks awarded for the question. Calculate how long you can afford to spend on each question and do not spend more time on it.

1 Principles of Double-entry Book-keeping

1.1 Introduction

Book-keeping is concerned with recording business transactions. The principle of double-entry book-keeping is based upon every transaction having two aspects or two parts, and for this reason two entries are made in the books of account in respect of each transaction.

Entries are made in a business's books of account, whether they be hand-written or computerised, by setting up various accounts and making debit and credit entries to those accounts. These terms are abbreviated to Dr. (debit) and Cr. (credit). Debits and credits can be likened to pluses and minuses or positives and negatives, which, in fact, is exactly what they are in computerised systems.

What we must do when making accounting entries is to decide (a) which accounts are affected and (b) whether the entries to those accounts are debit or credit. It is the basic principle of double-entry book-keeping that the answer to the above questions will always result in the amounts being debited to an account (or accounts) being equal to the amounts being credited to another account (or accounts). In order to formulate rules for debits and credits, we must categorise the accounts we keep into types of account.

1.2 Types of account

(a) Assets

Assets are things which we own — for example, buildings, motor vehicles and cash. Debtors are also an asset, since they represent something of value to the business — that is, an amount due to it.

(b) Liabilities

Liabilities are amounts owed by the business to other people.

(c) Expense

Expense accounts include such things as rent, electricity and purchases of goods for resale.

(d) Income

Income accounts record amounts of revenue to the business, such as sales, rents receivable and commission receivable.

1.3   Rules of double-entry book-keeping

Since the double-entry system is at the heart of book-keeping, you should understand the rules for it and commit them to memory.

Type of account	debit	credit
Assets/Expenses	to increase	to decrease
Liabilities/Income	to decrease	to increase

Let us now apply these rules to some typical business transactions.

(i) The owner starts the business by introducing £5,000, which he pays into a business bank account. The entry is

Dr. bank (an asset) to increase it
   Cr. capital (a liability) to increase it

The capital account represents the owner's account with the business. The concept may seem strange at first, but you must remember that you are keeping the books of the business, *not* the owner's personal books, and the capital introduced by the owner is amount due to the owner from the business.

(ii) The business purchases goods for resale, paying by cheque £1,000:

Dr. purchases (an expense) to increase it
   Cr. bank (an asset) to decrease it

(iii) The business purchases goods for resale on credit to the value of £2,000 from A. Brown:

Dr. purchases (an expense) to increase it
   Cr. A. Brown (a liability) to increase it

(iv) The business sells goods for cash £500:

Dr. bank (an asset) to increase it
   Cr. sales (an income) to increase it

The table below gives some further examples.

Transaction	Account to be debited	Account to be credited
Sold goods on credit to B. Jones: £600	B. Jones	Sales
Bought van for cash: £1,500	Van	Cash
Bought desk on credit from Office Supplies Ltd: £200	Office Furniture	Office Supplies Ltd
Paid wages	Wages	Cash
Paid rent by cheque: £200	Rent	Bank
Sold goods on credit to C. White: £300	C. White	Sales
Paid electricity bill by cheque: £50	Electricity	Bank
C. White paid the amount owing by him by cheque: £300	Bank	C. White

Make sure that you have understood how the rules have been applied to each of the above transactions before proceeding.

1.4 An illustration of the account

The ledger account is divided into two sides — a left-hand side, the debit side, and a right-hand side, the credit side. The name of the account must be clearly stated at the top. Below is the bank account as it would appear using the transactions in Section 1.3.

Dr.		Bank account			Cr.
Date	£		Date		£
Jan. 6 Capital	5,000		Jan. 7 Purchases		1,000
Jan. 8 Sales	500		Jan. 11 Rent		250
Jan. 15 C. White	300		Jan. 13 Electricity		50

You should notice how each side has a column to record the following:

(i) The date.
(ii) The name of the account to which the opposite entry is made — that is, the account credited where the bank account is debited and the account debited where the bank account is credited.
(iii) The amount or figures column. In practice this would record pounds and pence, but the pence have been omitted here for illustrative purposes.

The headings 'Dr.' and 'Cr.', while shown here, are often omitted in practice and are therefore usually not shown in the remainder of the book.

1.5 Balancing off the account

So far we have recorded debit and credit entries on our account. Looking to the bank account in Section 1.4 above, we cannot readily see the balance of our bank account. A computerised system will usually print the balance of the account after each transaction, but in a manual system we must calculate the balance, or balance off the account, as we call it.

Looking again to the bank account in Section 1.4, we can total each side of the account and calculate that

debit entries total £5,800
credit entries total £1,300

Debit entries therefore exceed credit entries by £4,500 (£5,800 less £1,300). We can say, then, that the account has a debit balance of £4,500. If the total of credit entries exceeds the total of debit entries, then the account has a credit balance.

The balancing-off process will now be described. On the credit side of the account we write the amount of the debit balance with the description 'balance c/d' (c/d = carried down). Next the entries are totalled for both the debit side and the credit side. These totals should be equal, since the amount written in as balance on the credit side was calculated to achieve just that. Finally, the balance which we have calculated is written in on the appropriate side of the account (that is to say, a debit balance on the debit side) with the description 'balance b/d' (b/d = brought down).

The above process is now illustrated.

Bank account

Date		£	Date		£
Jan. 6	Capital	5,000	Jan. 7	Purchases	1,000
Jan. 8	Sales	500	Jan. 11	Rent	250
Jan. 11	C. White	300	Jan. 13	Electricity	50
			Jan. 15	Balance c/d	4,500
		5,800			5,800
Jan. 16	Balance b/d	4,500			

Notice how the balance is usually carried down at the close of business on one day, and brought down at the start of business on the next day.

1.6 Purchases and sales returns

A purchases returns account is used to record the value of goods returned by a business to its suppliers. When goods are returned, the creditor's account is debited in order to decrease the liability to him and the purchases returns account is credited.

The sales returns account is used to record the value of goods returned to a business by its customers. When goods are returned, the debtor's account is credited in order to decrease the asset and the sales returns account is debited.

1.7 Worked example

Example 1.1

We shall now look at a typical examination question and illustrate how the entries will appear in the books of account.

1 December	B. Brown started business with £5,000 in a bank account.		

His purchases of stock on credit during the month were:

		£
8 December	T. Smith	400
12 December	R. Gray	300
19 December	B. Coals	140

His sales of stock on credit during the month were:

		£
8 December	R. Pike	600
20 December	T. Trout	700
29 December	R. Pike	400

Cash sales during the month, all paid into the bank, totalled £900. Other purchases and payments by cheque were:

		£
8 December	Rent	40
19 December	Electricity	130
	Motor van	1,000
20 December	Packing paper	140

29 December   R. Pike settled his account in full by cheque and Brown paid Smith, Gray and Coals in full by cheque. Brown purchased additional furniture and fittings on credit from Office Supplies Ltd for £500.

Solution 1.1

Capital

			£					£
				Dec. 1	Bank	(1)		5,000

Bank

			£					£
Dec. 1	Capital	(1)	5,000	Dec. 8	Rent	(9)		40
Dec. 31	Sales	(8)	900	Dec. 19	Electricity	(10)		130
Dec. 29	R. Pike	(13)	1,000	Dec. 19	Motor van	(11)		1,000
				Dec. 20	Packing paper	(12)		140
				Dec. 29	T. Smith	(14)		400
				Dec. 29	R. Gray	(15)		300
				Dec. 29	B. Coals	(16)		140

Purchases

			£			£
Dec. 8	T. Smith	(2)	400			
Dec. 12	R. Gray	(3)	300			
Dec. 19	B. Coals	(4)	140			

T. Smith

			£				£
Dec. 29	Bank	(14)	400	Dec. 8	Purchases	(2)	400

R. Gray

			£				£
Dec. 29	Bank	(15)	300	Dec. 12	Purchases	(3)	300

B. Coals

			£				£
Dec. 29	Bank	(16)	140	Dec. 19	Purchases	(4)	140

Sales

			£					£
				Dec. 8	R. Pike	(5)		600
				Dec. 20	T. Trout	(6)		700
				Dec. 29	R. Pike	(7)		400
				Dec. 31	Cash	(8)		900

R. Pike

			£				£
Dec. 8	Sales	(5)	600	Dec. 29	Bank	(13)	1,000
Dec. 29	Sales	(7)	400				

T. Trout

			£		£
Dec. 20	Sales	(6)	700		

Rent

			£		£
Dec. 8	Bank	(9)	40		

Electricity

			£		£
Dec. 19	Bank	(10)	130		

Motor van

			£		£
Dec. 19	Bank	(11)	1,000		

Packing paper

			£		£
Dec. 20	Bank	(12)	140		

Furniture and fittings

			£		£
Dec. 29	Office Supplies Ltd	(17)	500		

Office Supplies Ltd

			£					£
				Dec. 29	Furniture and fittings	(17)		500

You should notice how the entry records the following: (a) the date; (b) the other account to which an entry is made; (c) the reference (you should use this to understand the entries); and (d) the amount.

1.8 Further exercises

Question 1.1

Marion decides to open a boutique and rents a shop for the purpose. The following are her business transactions.

Jan. 7   She pays £4,000 into a business bank account
Jan. 8   She pays £3,000 for fixtures and fittings for the shop
Jan. 10 She buys on credit clothes costing £2,600 from Wholesale Clothing Ltd
Jan. 11 She pays into the bank the first week's takings of £1,650

Jan. 12	She buys more clothes on credit from Good Supplies Ltd £1,100
Jan. 14	She pays rent of £1,100
Jan. 18	She pays into the bank the second week's takings of £1,800
Jan. 20	She pays an electricity bill of £50 by cheque
Jan. 21	She pays £40 for stationery
Jan. 25	She banks the week's takings of £1,295
Jan. 28	She pays Wholesale Clothing Ltd the amount due to them
Jan. 29	She returns soiled clothes to Good Supplies Ltd £50
Jan. 31	She values stock of clothes at cost £1,000

Set out all of the accounts in the books of Marion's boutique business and balance off the bank account.

Answer 1.1

Bank

		£			£
Jan. 7	Capital	4,000	Jan. 8	Fittings and furniture	3,000
Jan. 11	Sales	1,650	Jan. 16	Rent	1,100
Jan. 18	Sales	1,800	Jan. 20	Electricity	50
Jan. 25	Sales	1,295	Jan. 21	Stationery	40
			Jan. 28	Wholesale Clothing	2,600
			Jan. 31	Balance c/d	1,955
		8,745			8,745
Feb. 1	Balance b/d	1,955			

Wholesale Clothing

		£			£
Jan. 28	Bank	2,600	Jan. 10	Purchases	2,600

Sales

	£			£
		Jan. 11	Bank	1,650
		Jan. 18	Bank	1,800
		Jan. 25	Bank	1,295

Rent

		£		£
Jan. 14	Bank	1,100		

Capital

	£			£
		Jan. 7	Bank	4,000

Fittings and furniture

		£		£
Jan. 8	Bank	3,000		

Purchases

		£		£
Jan. 10	Wholesale Clothing	2,600		
Jan. 12	Good Supplies Ltd	1,100		

Purchases returns

		£				£
			Jan. 12	Good Supplies Ltd		50

Good Supplies Ltd

		£				£
Jan. 12	Purchases returns	50	Jan. 12	Purchases		1,100

Electricity

		£			£
Jan. 20	Bank	50			

Stationery

		£			£
Jan. 21	Bank	40			

Question 1.2

Enter the following transactions into the books of D. Margrave for the month of September.

Sept. 1   Cash in hand £150

Sept. 2   Bought £350 of goods on credit from C. Russell

Sept. 3   Paid electricity £40

Sept. 4   Cash sales £140

Sept. 5   Paid wages £80

Sept. 11   Cash takings £165

Sept. 15   Bought office furniture £60

Sept. 18   Cash sales £150

Sept. 21   Sold goods to P. Lynch on credit £50

Sept. 25   Paid advertising £50

Sept. 27   Cash sales £140

Answer 1.2

Cash

		£			£
Sept. 1	Capital	150	Sept. 3	Electricity	40
Sept. 4	Sales	140	Sept. 5	Wages	80
Sept. 11	Sales	165	Sept. 15	Office furniture	60
Sept. 18	Sales	150	Sept. 25	Advertising	50
Sept. 27	Sales	140	Sept. 30	Balance c/d	515
		745			745
Oct. 1	Balance b/d	515			

Capital

		£			£
			Sept. 1	Cash	150

C. Russell

		£			£
			Sept. 2	Purchases	350

			Purchases			
			£			£
Sept. 2	C. Russell	350				

			Electricity			
			£			£
Sept. 3	Cash	40				

			Sales			
		£				£
			Sept. 4	Cash		140
			Sept. 11	Cash		165
			Sept. 18	Cash		150
			Sept. 21	P. Lynch		50
			Sept. 27	Cash		140

			Wages			
		£				£
Sept. 5	Cash	80				

			Office furniture			
		£				£
Sept. 15	Cash	60				

			P. Lynch			
		£				£
Sept. 21	Sales	50				

			Advertising			
		£				£
Sept. 25	Cash	50				

Note: The reason for only balancing off the cash account at this stage will become clear in the following chapters.

2 The Trial Balance

2.1 Introduction

So far we have concerned ourselves with the posting of transactions to the ledger accounts, and we have seen how we balance off the cash account. The next stage in the book-keeping process is to examine the balances which exist on all of the accounts which we have opened. Looking to worked example 1.1 in Chapter 1, we shall now examine the balance on each of the accounts in the books of B. Brown.

(a) Capital

There is only one entry on this account, a credit entry for £5,000. Hence, the account has a credit balance of £5,000, representing the liability of the business to the owner.

(b) Bank

The debit entries total £6,900, as compared with credit entries totalling £2,150. If we deduct £2,150 from £6,900, we arrive at £4,750, which is the debit balance on the account representing the amount of money which, according to our records, we have in our bank account.

(c) Purchases

There are three debit entries totalling £840. A debit balance of £840 representing our total purchases to date.

(d) T. Smith

On this account the amount of the debit entry equals the amount of the credit entry. We can therefore say that the account has a nil balance. This reflects the fact that there is now neither an amount owing to T. Smith nor an amount owing from T. Smith, since we purchased goods from him and at a later date we settled that debt.

(e) R. Gray

Exactly the same comments apply as for T. Smith.

(f) B. Coals

Exactly the same comments apply as for R. Gray and T. Smith.

(g) Sales

The credit entries totalling £2,600 with no debit entries means a credit balance of £2,600, reflecting our total sales to date, both for cash and on credit.

(h) R. Pike

As with T. Smith's account, the debit entries in total equal the credit entry and there is therefore a nil balance on the account, reflecting the fact that after the transactions entered there is neither an amount owing to nor an amount owing from R. Pike.

(i) T. Trout

A single debit entry of £700 on this account means that there is a debit balance of £700, representing the amount due from T. Trout – i.e. T. Trout is a debtor for that amount to the business.

(j) Rent

A single debit entry of £40 means that there is a debit balance of £40, representing the total expense on this item during this period.

(k) Electricity

The same comments apply as for rent. A debit balance of £130, representing the amount spent on electricity during the period.

(l) Motor Van

A debit balance of £1,000 represents the book value of the asset motor van.

(m) Packing Paper

Another expense account, this time with a debit balance of £140, representing the business's expenditure on this item.

(n) Furniture and Fittings

A debit balance of £500, representing the book value of the asset furniture and fittings.

(o) Office Supplies Ltd

A credit balance of £500, representing the liability of the business to Office Supplies Ltd.

2.2 Purpose of the trial balance

Having ascertained the balance on our various accounts, we are now in a position to progress a stage further in the book-keeping process.

You will recall from the first chapter that the whole basis of double-entry book-keeping is a system of debit and credit entries of equal amounts. If we have adhered to this rule, it should be obvious that if we list the debit and credit balances the totals of each should be equal. This is the whole purpose of the trial balance — to check the arithmetical accuracy of our book-keeping. If our totals of debit balances and credit balances are equal (i.e. our trial balance agrees), then we have proved the arithmetical accuracy of our book-keeping.

You should note two things in particular regarding the trial balance.

(i) It is *not* part of the double-entry system of book-keeping.
(ii) The following errors will *not* be revealed by the trial balance: (a) a posting of the correct amount to the correct side of an account but to the wrong account; (b) a posting of the wrong amount to both the debit of one account and the credit of another (provided that it is the same wrong amount in both cases); (c) failure to enter a transaction anywhere in the books.

The subject of errors is dealt with fully in Chapter 8.

2.3 Worked examples

Example 2.1

From the books of B. Brown illustrated in Chapter 1 prepare the trial balance of B. Brown's business as at 31 December.

Solution 2.1

	Dr £	Cr. £
Capital		5,000
Bank	4,750	
Purchases	840	
Sales		2,600
T. Trout	700	
Rent	40	
Electricity	130	
Motor van	1,000	
Packing paper	140	
Furniture and fittings	500	
Office Supplies Ltd		500
	£8,100	£8,100

You should notice:

(i) The debit balances and credit balances both total £8,100 − i.e. our trial balance agrees and thus the arithmetical accuracy of our book-keeping has been proved.

(ii) The accounts with a nil balance (e.g. T. Smith) have been omitted, since these can now be considered closed.

Example 2.2

The following were the balances in the books of G. Green as at 31 March 1985, omitting the capital account. You are asked to prepare the trial balance at 31 March 1985, the capital account being included as the balancing figure.

	£
Bank overdraft	2,416
Heating	213
Sales	16,134
Purchases	11,210
Commission income	1,367
Cash in hand	110
Debtors	4,130
Creditors	2,695
Owner's drawings	600
Postage and stationery	715
Premises	26,900
Repairs to buildings	620

Note: There are two or three new accounts mentioned here, but you should be able to work out whether they are debit or credit balances from the rules which you have already learned.

Solution 2.2

	Dr. £	Cr. £
Bank overdraft (1)		2,416
Heating	213	
Sales		16,134
Purchases	11,210	
Commissions received		1,367
Cash in hand	110	
Debtors	4,130	
Creditors		2,695
Owner's drawings (2)	600	
Postage and stationery	715	
Premises	26,900	
Repairs to buildings	620	
Capital (3)		21,886
	£44,498	£44,498

NOTES

(1) Bank overdraft is a liability to the bank − i.e. a credit balance.

(2) Owner's drawings represents money withdrawn from the business by the owner − i.e. he becomes a debtor of the business for this amount although it will usually be set off later against his capital.

(3) Balancing figure as required in the question.

You should notice how the debit balances are either (a) assets (e.g. premises, debtors, cash) or (b) expenses (e.g. heating, purchases, repairs) and also that credit balances are either (a) liabilities (e.g. creditors) or (b) income (e.g. sales, commission received).

2.4 Further exercises

Question 2.1

From the books of Marion's boutique in Question 1.1 in Chapter 1 extract a trial balance as at 31 January 1985.

Answer 2.1

Trial balance of Marion's boutique at 31 January 1985

	Dr. £	Cr. £
Bank	1,955	
Wholesale Clothing	—	
Sales		4,745
Rent	1,100	
Capital		4,000
Furniture and fittings	3,000	
Purchases	3,700	
Purchases returns		50
Good Supplies Ltd		1,050
Electricity	50	
Stationery	40	
	£9,845	£9,845

Question 2.2

From the books of D. Margrave in Question 1.2 in Chapter 1 extract a trial balance as at 30 September 1985.

Answer 2.2

Trial balance of D. Margrave at 30 September 1985

	Dr. £	Cr. £
Cash	515	
Capital		150
C. Russell		350
Purchases	350	
Electricity	40	
Sales		645
Wages	80	
Office furniture	60	
P. Lynch	50	
Advertising	50	
	£1,145	£1,145

3 Trading and Profit and Loss Accounts

3.1   Explanation

The trading and profit and loss account is prepared to calculate and show in detail the profit or loss for an accounting period of the business. It is divided into two sections (or accounts) — the trading section and the profit and loss section.

3.2   The trading section

The trading section shows the gross profit, which is the difference between sales and cost of goods sold or cost of sales. The sales figure will be the value of sales to the customers of the business, as posted to the credit of the sales account in the ledger and transferred to the trading and profit and loss account. The value of any goods returned by customers, as posted to the sales returns account, will be deducted from the total sales figure to arrive at a net sales figure.

The cost of goods sold requires further consideration. If a business sells all the stock which it purchases during a trading period, then the cost of goods sold is the amount paid for purchases of goods for resale. Where, however, the business has stock remaining at the end of a period, we must deduct this closing stock valuation from our purchases to arrive at a cost of goods sold figure. We now have

Purchases	x
less closing stock	(x)
Cost of goods sold	T

The closing stock of a business is available to sell in the following accounting period and we must therefore include the closing stock figure in the following period's cost of goods sold calculation. The calculation then would be for the next period's cost of goods sold figure

Opening stock (last period's closing stock)	x
add purchases	x
sub-total	S/T
less closing stock	(x)
Cost of goods sold	T

We have not yet examined the purchases figure. The purchases figure will be the value of purchases of goods for resale from suppliers, less the value of any goods returned to those suppliers. Additionally, it should include the cost of bringing those goods to their existing state and condition; a common example of such a cost would be carriage inwards.

3.3 The profit and loss section

The profit and loss section shows the net profit of the business, which is defined as

gross profit
add other income (e.g. rents, commission)
less other expenses (not included in cost of goods sold)

Other expenses will be selling and administrative expenses.

3.4 Preparation of trading, profit and loss account

We have seen how the gross profit and net profit are calculated, which it is important to understand. However, you must also understand the mechanics of the preparation of a trading and profit and loss account using the double-entry system of book-keeping. It is important to note that this account is part of the double-entry system.

We have already seen that we need the values from the following accounts to calculate gross and then net profit: sales, purchases, carriage inwards, income accounts and expense accounts. The rule is that we must transfer to the trading and profit and loss account the balance on all expense and income accounts — i.e. all accounts which are not asset or liability accounts (look back to Section 1.2 if you are not clear on these definitions).

We can now illustrate how two of these accounts will now appear in the ledger, using the example in Chapter 1.

Purchases

1985		£	1985		£
Dec. 8	T. Smith	400	Dec. 31	Trading account	840
Dec. 12	R. Gray	300			
Dec. 19	B. Coals	140			
		£840			£840

Electricity

1985		£	1985		£
Dec. 19	Bank	130	Dec. 31	Profit and loss account	130
		£130			£130

From the above it can be seen that accounts with debit balances will appear as a debit entry on the trading and profit and loss account. Accounts with a credit balance will appear as a credit entry on the trading and profit and loss account.

Finally, we must consider the entries to record the closing stock valuation. The entry which you may find easier to remember rather than work out the reasons for is

Dr. Stock
    Cr. Trading account

We debit stock, because we want to record an asset on the books (remember debit an asset to increase it). The explanation of the credit entry is that by recognising the closing stock we are reducing our cost of goods sold and thus increasing our income. Our stock account will then appear as follows:

Stock

	£
Dec. 31 Trading account	100

The debit balance remains on the stock account until the end of the next trading period, when it is transferred to the debit of that year's trading and profit and loss account.

When the net profit has been calculated, which will be the balance on the profit and loss account after posting all expenses and income, we transfer that profit to the owner's capital account. The entry is then

Dr. Profit and loss account
Cr. Capital account

3.5 Other trading account expenses

So far we have recorded in the trading account the cost of purchases as adjusted by the opening and closing stocks, and in the case of a simple trading business this will be all that is entered in that account. However, any costs incurred in bringing goods into a saleable condition and to their place of sale should be charged to the trading account. Such items will include carriage inwards, warehouse costs and packing costs. It is important, therefore, to know the type of business for which we are preparing accounts, in order to decide whether expenses are (a) trading account items, which will be included in the cost of sales calculation and affect gross profit, or (b) profit and loss account items, which affect only the net profit.

We shall now work through some examples, which you should study carefully: in particular, note the differences between the alternative presentations.

3.6 Worked examples

Example 3.1

From the trial balance produced in Section 2.3 prepare a trading and profit and loss account of B. Brown for the year ended 31 December 1985. Closing stock is £200.

Solution 3.1

Trading and profit and loss account of B. Brown for year ended 31 December 1985

	£		£
Purchases	840	Sales	2,600
Packing	140	Closing stock	200
Gross profit c/d	1,820		
	£2,800		£2,800

Rent		40	Gross profit b/d	1,820
Electricity		130		
Net profit (transferred to capital account)		1,650		
		£1,820		£1,820

Alternatively, we could prepare the account in vertical format to make it more readable for non-accountants. It would then appear as follows:

Trading and profit and loss account of B. Brown for year ended 31 December 1985

		£
Sales		2,600
Purchases	840	
less closing stock	200	
	640	
Packing paper	140	
Cost of goods sold		780
Gross profit		1,820
less		
Rent	40	
Electricity	130	170
Net profit		£1,650

Example 3.2

From the following trial balance, taken from the books of G. Green at 31 December 1985, prepare a trading and profit and loss account. Closing stock at 31 December 1985 is £1,000.

	Dr. £	Cr. £
Sales		6,000
Sales returns	500	
Capital		7,000
Motor vehicle	5,700	
Purchases	3,500	
Purchases returns		400
Carriage inwards	610	
Carriage outwards	405	
Rates	1,000	
Insurance	40	
Debtors	500	
Drawings	300	
Creditors		300
Bank	45	
Opening stock 1 January 1985	1,100	
	£13,700	£13,700

Solution 3.2

Trading and profit and loss account of G. Green for year ending 31 December 1985

		£
Sales (£6,000−500)		5,500
Opening stock		1,100
Purchases (£3,500−400)	3,100	
add Carriage inwards	610	3,710
		4,810
less Closing stock		1,000
Cost of goods sold		3,810
Gross profit		1,690
less		
Carriage outwards (1)	405	
Rates	1,000	
Insurance	40	1,445
Net profit (transferred to capital)		£245

NOTE

(1) Carriage outwards is a selling expense and therefore appears in the profit and loss section of the account.

3.7 Further exercise

Question 3.1

From the following trial balance, taken from the books of Darren Guymer, draw up a trading and profit and loss account for the year ending 30 November 1985.

	Dr. £	Cr. £
Capital		50,000
Cash at bank	6,000	
Cash in hand	104	
Debtors	15,000	
Creditors		14,150
Stock (1 Dec. 1984)	40,000	
Motor van	8,000	
Sales		210,000
Purchases	194,621	
Purchases returns		610
Sales returns	650	
Carriage	150	
Carriage outwards	410	
Telephone	805	
Insurance	610	
Sundry expenses	410	
Wages	8,000	
	£274,760	£274,760

Stock at 30 November 1985 was £74,100

Answer 3.1

Gross profit £49,289
Net profit £39,054

20

4 Balance Sheet

4.1   Purpose

We saw in Chapter 3 that the trading and profit and loss account is prepared to show the profit or loss of the business for an accounting period. The balance sheet is prepared to show the financial position of the business at the end of that accounting period. To achieve this we show the amounts on the asset and liability accounts in the books of the business. You should note that it is not part of the double-entry system; the balances on the asset and liability accounts are carried forward to the next accounting period, as illustrated in Section 1.5 for the bank account. Before preparing the balance sheet, all of the asset and liability accounts should be balanced off as illustrated there.

4.2   Preparation of the balance sheet

In order to prepare a balance sheet in good format, we must consider the asset and liability accounts under certain headings and terms which we must understand and be able to define. We shall now look at those terms.

(a) Capital

We learned in Section 1.2 that capital is a liability account and, in the widest sense of the word, it is a liability representing the liability of the business to the owner. In other words, it is the owner's investment in the business. Because of this latter definition, often, when we talk about liabilities, we mean only liabilities to third parties and not the owner's capital account.

As we have already seen, an entry is made to the capital account when the owner introduces capital into the business. In Chapter 3 we saw another instance requiring a posting to the capital account — that is, when the profit and loss account is closed and the balance is transferred to the owner's capital account. The only other occasion when this account is posted to is when the owner withdraws cash or stock from the business. If cash is withdrawn, the entry is

Dr. Capital (to reduce the liability account)
   Cr. Cash (to reduce the asset cash)

If stock is withdrawn, the entry is

Dr. Capital (to reduce the liability account)
   Cr. Purchases (to reduce the expense)

An alternative to making the posting direct to the capital account is to debit a drawings account and to transfer the balance from the drawings account at the end of the accounting period to the capital account.

It is worth noting that the three instances mentioned above are the only occasions where entries are made to the capital account. In summary, they are: (a) when the owner introduces capital; (b) when the profit and loss account is closed by transferring the balance (net profit) to the capital account; (c) when the owner withdraws cash or stock from the business.

(b) Current Liabilities

Current liabilities represent amounts payable within a period of 12 months from the balance sheet date. They will include bank overdrafts, since banks reserve the right to demand immediate payment.

(c) Long-term Liabilities

Long-term liabilities represent amounts payable more than 12 months after the balance sheet date.

(d) Fixed Assets

Fixed assets are those assets which are held for continuing use in the business with a view to profits being earned from that use. Examples are premises, fixtures and fittings, and motor vehicles.

(e) Current Assets

We can define current assets as assets which we intend to turn into cash within a relatively short period of time or which are already cash, including bank balances. Examples are stock, debtors and bank balances.

(f) Working Capital or Net Current Assets

Working capital is defined as current assets less current liabilities, and, as will be explained in Chapter 20, is an important figure in comprehending and interpreting balance sheets.

(g) Net Assets

Net assets represent the difference between total assets and liabilities to third parties. They will therefore be equivalent to fixed assets plus working capital.

4.3 Balance sheet equation

Because we have followed the double-entry system of book-keeping as described in Chapter 1, if our books are arithmetically correct, the following equation will be true:

capital + liabilities = assets

or, rewritten,

capital = assets less liabilities

While we follow the double-entry system of book-keeping this equation will always be true. In the worked examples which follow you should notice how it is true for those answers. Also compare and note the differences between the two formats.

4.4   Capital and revenue expenditure

We have so far mentioned that expense account balances are transferred to the profit and loss account and that asset account balances are carried forward to the next accounting period. Since the profit calculation will change if we classify an item wrongly as either an expense or an asset, the importance of correct classification cannot be over-emphasised. In order that the account be treated correctly, we must accurately classify initial expenditure as either capital or revenue expenditure.

Capital expenditure is the money spent on buying fixed assets or adding to their value. Revenue expenditure is the money spent on running the business on a day-to-day basis. For example, building an extension on to an existing building is capital expenditure; repairing the roof would be revenue expenditure. Capital expenditure is debited to a fixed asset account which appears on the balance sheet, whereas revenue expenditure is debited to an expense account which is transferred to the profit and loss account.

4.5   Worked examples

Example 4.1

From the trial balance produced in Section 2.3 prepare a balance sheet for **B. Brown** as at 31 December 1985.

Solution 4.1

Balance sheet of B. Brown as at 31 December 1985

	£			£
Capital balance 1 Jan. 1985	5,000	Fixed assets		
add net profit	1,650	Furniture and fittings		500
Capital balance 31 Dec. 1985	6,650	Motor van		1,000
				1,500
Current liabilities		Current assets		
Creditors	500	Stock	200	
		Debtors	700	
		Bank	4,750	5,650
	£7,150			£7,150

Alternatively — again for better presentation and for the benefit of non-accountants having to read balance sheets — we could prepare it in a vertical format.

Balance sheet of B. Brown as at 31 December 1985

Fixed assets		£
Furniture and fittings		500
Motor van		1,000
		1,500
Current assets		
Stocks	200	
Debtors	700	
Bank	4,750	
	5,650	
less Current liabilities		
Creditors	500	
Working capital		5,150
Net assets		£6,650
Financed by		
Capital balance 1 Jan. 1985		5,000
add net profit		1,650
Capital balance 31 Dec. 1985		£6,650

Example 4.2

From the trial balance given in Example 3.2 of Chapter 3, prepare a balance sheet for
G. Green as at 31 December 1985.

Solution 4.2

Balance sheet of G. Green as at 31 December 1985

Fixed assets		£
Motor vehicle		5,700
Current assets		
Stock	1,000	
Debtors	500	
Bank	45	
	1,545	
less Current liabilities		
Creditors	300	
Working capital		1,245
		£6,945
Capital balance 1 Jan. 1985		7,000
add net profit		245
		7,245
less drawings		300
Capital balance 31 Dec. 1985		£6,945

4.6   Further exercises

Question 4.1

From the trial balance given in Question 3.1 of Chapter 3 prepare a balance sheet of Darren Guymer at 30 November 1985.

Answer 4.1

Fixed assets £8,000
Current assets £95,204
Current liabilities £14,150
Capital £89,054

Question 4.2

(a) Explain the meaning of each of the following terms:
 (i) 'capital expenditure';
 (ii) 'revenue expenditure'.   *[3 marks]*
(b) Give **two** examples of each type of expenditure given in (a) above.   *[4 marks]*
(c) Devise a suitable example to explain the effect on the final accounts of incorrectly classifying an item of capital expenditure as revenue.   *[4 marks]*
(d) Explain the significance to the preparation of final accounts of being able to distinguish between capital and revenue expenditure.   *[4 marks]*
                                                                   (AEB)

Answer 4.2

(a) Refer to Section 4.4.
(b) (i) Premises, motor van;   (ii) wages, electricity.
(c) Refer to Section 4.4. For example, if the cost of a new motor van were treated as an expense, this would reduce profit by that amount. When it is treated correctly as capital expenditure, it is shown as an asset in the balance sheet and has no effect upon the net profit.
(d) Refer to Section 4.4 and (c) above.

5 Cash Book and Cash Discounts

5.1　Cash book

The cash book in manual systems and some computerised systems is a book combining the cash account and the bank account. (Other uses will be discussed in Chapter 7.) Refer back to Section 1.4, where a bank account was illustrated, and compare the cash and bank accounts with the illustration below, where we have a separate column for cash and bank.

Cash book

		Cash £	Bank £			Cash £	Bank £
Jan. 1	Balance b/d	100	5,000	Jan. 8	Wages	150	
Jan. 6	Sales	800		Jan. 9	Rent		600
Jan. 7	D. Taylor		510	Jan. 11	J. Small		750
				Jan. 15	Balances c/d	750	4,160
		900	5,510			900	5,510
Jan. 16	Balance b/d	750	4,160				

Make sure that you understand this illustration before proceeding. The entries to the credit columns for cash and bank represent payments by cash and cheque, respectively. The entries to the debit columns represent receipts of cash and payments direct into the bank account by cheque or other means. The balances represent the cash held by the business and the balance at the bank.

We can now go on to consider the entries where cash is paid into the bank or withdrawn from the bank.

Withdrawal of cash from the bank will increase our cash balance and decrease our bank balance, and the entry is

> Dr. Cash account
> 　Cr. Bank account

Cash paid into the bank will increase our bank balance and decrease our cash balance and the entry is

> Dr. Bank account
> 　Cr. Cash account

We can illustrate this by continuing our previous example and making an entry to record the paying in of £500 to our bank account from our cash in hand.

		Cash £	Bank £			Cash £	Bank £
Jan. 16	Balance b/d	750	4,160	Jan. 17	Bank	500	
Jan. 17	Cash		500	Jan. 18	Balance b/d	250	4,660
		750	4,660			750	4,660
Jan. 18	Balance b/d	250	4,660				

5.2 Cash discounts

Cash discounts fall into two categories — discounts allowed and discounts received. Discounts allowed occur where we accept a payment from a customer of a lesser amount than the amount due, because the customer has paid us promptly. Discounts received occur where a supplier allows us to pay a lesser amount to him than the amount due, because we have paid him promptly.

There are two reasons why businesses allow discounts. First, they improve their own cash flow — i.e. prevent it going into an overdraft situation — or release funds for investment elsewhere. Second, they reduce the possibility of bad debts: the more quickly payments are received the less chance there is of debtors becoming unable to pay.

When a business allows a discount, it nonetheless needs to reduce the debtor's account by the full amount of the debt being settled. In addition to the debit to cash or bank and the credit to the debtor's account, the following entry is necessary to completely eliminate the balance from the debtor's account:

Dr. Discounts allowed account
Cr. Debtor's account

At the end of the accounting period the balance on the discounts allowed account is transferred to the profit and loss account and treated as an expense of the business, thus reducing the profit. Conversely, when a business receives a discount, the creditor's account needs to be reduced by the full amount of the debt due and the following entry then becomes necessary:

Dr. Creditor's account
Cr. Discounts received account

At the end of the accounting period the balance on the discounts received account is transferred to the profit and loss account as other income and increases the profit.

5.3 Cash discounts in the cash book

Because of the frequency with which discounts allowed and received occur, we do not usually make separate entries in our books every time they occur. The usual method is to add an additional column to the cash book illustrated in Section 5.1. On the debit side we create a column 'discounts allowed' and enter amounts into this column as they occur. When the credit entry is made to the debtor's account, we post the full amount of the debt — i.e. the cash received plus the discount allowed to the credit of the debtor's account. On the credit side we create a column 'discounts received' and enter amounts into this column as they occur. When the debit entry is made to the creditor's account, we post the full amount of the debt — i.e. the cash paid plus the discount received to the debit of the creditor's account.

The discount columns are not part of the double-entry system. In so far as discounts allowed are concerned, we have so far debited our cash or bank account with the amount actually received and credited the debtor with the full amount due. It now remains to post the discount to the debit of the discounts allowed account, and this we do in one total amount at the end of a period. Similarly, we must total discounts received and post these to the credit of the discounts received account. This completes the double entry, which we can summarise for cash received from debtors as

Dr. Bank account (with amount received)
Dr. Discounts allowed account (with the discount allowed)
   Cr. Debtor's account (with the amount received plus the discount)

Similarly, we can summarise the entries for payment to creditors as

Dr.   Creditor's account (with the amount paid plus the discount allowed)
   Cr. Discount received account (with the amount of the discount received)
   Cr. Bank (with the amount actually paid)

5.4   Petty cash

In businesses other than the very small ones it becomes advantageous to maintain a petty-cash account in addition to the cash and bank accounts. The benefits are as follows: (a) the petty-cash duties can be delegated to a junior member of staff; (b) the main cash book does not become over-large because of a large quantity of small items; (c) an analysed petty-cash book can be maintained so that totals only for each category of expense will be posted to the various expense accounts — e.g. postage, stationery, etc.

Where such a book is maintained, the recommended system to operate is the imprest system. Under this system a float is established to meet requirements for the following period. At the end of that period the petty cashier is reimbursed with the amounts actually paid out, which restores the petty cash balance to the original float. From the control point of view, this system has the advantage that at any one time the total value of vouchers which have not been reimbursed plus the petty-cash balance will equal the agreed float.

5.5   Worked examples

Example 5.1

The cashier of your firm has been absent owing to illness and no entries have been made in the cash book for the period 24–30 November. The cash book has three columns — for discounts, cash and bank.

On 23 November the balances in the cash book were: cash in hand £86 and bank overdraft £380. There were no cash discount items in the cash book at that date. The following additional information is available:

Nov. 24   Paid cash for stationery £8 and stamps £11
     25   Sent L. Fairclough a cheque for £280 and took £20 cash discount
     26   Received and paid into bank a cheque from A. Tatlock £432 accepted in full settlement of his debt of £470
     28   Banked a cheque from E. Yates £506 on account and sold goods £262 on credit to K. Barlow
     29   Cashed a cheque £42 for office use
     30   Cash sales for the period 24–30 November, £544, paid direct to bank

At the start of business on 1 December there was £59 in the firm's cash box.

REQUIRED

(a) Preparation of the cash book for the period 24–30 November, bringing down the balances to 1 December.   [*10 marks*]

(b) An explanation of why you may be dissatisfied with the correctness of the cash balances.   [*1 mark*]

(c) An explanation of where discount allowed and discount received will be posted from the cash book and how each of them will affect the net profit calculation   (*2 marks*)   [*2 marks*]

Solution 5.1

(a)

Cash book

		Discount £	Cash £	Bank £			Discount £	Cash £	Bank £
Nov. 23	Balance b/d		86		Nov. 23	Balance b/d			380
Nov. 26	A. Tatlock	38		432	Nov. 24	Stationery		8	
Nov. 28	E. Yates			506		Postage		11	
Nov. 29	Bank		42		Nov. 25	L. Fairclough	20		280
Nov. 30	Sales			544	Nov. 29	Cash			42
					Nov. 30	Balance c/d		109	780
		38	128	1,482			20	128	1,482
Dec. 1	Balance b/d		109	780					

(b) Since at 1 December there is only £59 in the cash box either £50 (£109 − £59) has been spent and not recorded or it has been misappropriated.

(c) The £38 representing discount allowed will be posted to the debit of the discounts allowed account and will eventually be transferred to the profit and loss account as an expense, thus reducing the net profit. The £20 representing discounts received will be posted to the credit of the discounts received account and will eventually be transferred to the profit and loss account as an income item, thus increasing the net profit.

Example 5.2

The cashier of the firm in which you are employed has been absent through illness and no entries have been made in the three-column cash book for the period 25–31 January. On 1 February you are instructed to bring the entries up to date. You obtain the following information.

(a) At the close of business on 24 January the cash book balances were: office cash £156.70, bank £1,569.40 (debit). For the period 1–24 January the entries made in the discount allowed and discount received columns totalled £117.60 and £83.30, respectively.

(b) Some credit customers have settled their accounts by cheque and the cheques have been paid into the bank:

		Amount owed £	Cash discount deducted
25 January	G. Long	264.00	2½ per cent
28 January	D. Fender	276.00	2½ per cent
30 January	B. Keeper	148.00	5 per cent

(c) Payments made out of office cash:

		£
25 January	Travelling expenses	28.50
28 January	Postage stamps	12.60
29 January	Stationery	18.20

(d) Payments by cheque to settle trade creditors' accounts:

		Amount owed £	Cash discount deducted
25 January	N. Morris	1,065.40	Nil
26 January	F. Talbot	616.00	2½ per cent
30 January	J. Ford	419.50	Nil

(e) Other payments made by cheque:

		£
26 January	Telephone bill	175.30
26 January	Repairs to typewriter	43.40
29 January	Wages and salaries	1,360.60

(f) Cash sales are always paid intact into bank at the end of the day. The total for 25–31 January, which you can enter in one amount, was £3,600.45.

(g) At the start of business on 1 February there is £87.40 in the firm's cash box.

(h) A statement received from the bank shows a favourable balance of £2,591.65 at 31 January. There are no items in the statement of which you are not already aware, but you notice that the cheque sent to J. Ford on 30 January has not yet been cleared.

You are asked:

(1) to write up the firm's cash book for the period 25–31 January and carry down the balances;
(2) to say whether or not you are satisfied with the correctness of the cash and bank balances, giving your reasons.

Note: You are not required to make any postings to the ledger.

(OLE)

Solution 5.2

(1)
(see the top of page 31)
(2) We can be satisfied with the bank balance of £2,591.65, since when J. Ford's cheque is cleared, the balance will be reduced to £2,172.15, exactly as shown in the cash book. We cannot be satisfied with the cash balance, since at £97.40 it is £10 more than the cash in the cash box and £10 has therefore been spent and not recorded, or misappropriated.

Cash book

		Discounts	Cash	Bank			Discounts	Cash	Bank
		£	£	£			£	£	£
Jan. 24	Balances b/d	117.60	156.70	1,569.40	Jan. 24	Balance b/d	83.30		
Jan. 25	G. Long	6.60		257.40	Jan. 25	Travelling expenses		28.50	
Jan. 28	D. Fender	6.90		269.10	Jan. 26	N. Morris			1,065.40
Jan. 30	B. Keeper	7.40		140.60	Jan. 26	F. Talbot	15.40		600.60
Jan. 31	Sales			3,600.45	Jan. 26	Telephone			175.30
					Jan. 26	Equipment and repairs			43.40
					Jan. 28	Postage		12.60	
					Jan. 29	Stationery		18.20	
					Jan. 29	Wages and salaries			1,360.60
					Jan. 30	J. Ford			419.50
					Jan. 31	Balance c/d		97.40	2,172.15
		138.50	156.70	5,836.95			98.70	156.70	5,836.95
Feb. 1	Balance b/d		97.40	2,172.15					

Example 5.3

P. Black is in business as a retailer. On 1 May 1983 his balance sheet disclosed the following information:

Liabilities	£	Assets	£
Creditor W. Jones	410	Cash in hand	50
Capital	31,100	Cash at bank	2,050
		Stock	1,410
		Premises	28,000
	31,510		31,510

The following transactions took place during the month of May 1983:

May		£
2	Bought goods on credit from W. Jones	175
	Bought on credit new shop fittings from Shopfitters Ltd	1,000
3	Bought stock on credit from R. Wilkinson	450
6	Returned goods to W. Jones	34
	Paid W. Jones by cheque	410
	Cash sales to date	700
11	Personal drawings in cash	250
13	Banked	400
	Bought stationery for business use and paid cash	40
	Paid R. Wilkinson by cheque	450
	Cash sales to date. Banked immediately	540
	Calculations indicated that a sum of money had been stolen from the till	50

(a)   Open all necessary ledger accounts, including accounts for cash and bank (a two-column cash book will be accepted instead of separate accounts), enter the opening balances and record the above transactions.

(b)   Extract a trial balance on 14 May 1983.

(L)

Solution 5.3

(a)

Cash book

		Cash £	Bank £				Cash £	Bank £
May 1	Balance b/d	50	2,050	May 6	W. Jones			410
May 6	Sales	700		May 11	Drawings		250	
May 13	Cash		400	May 13	Bank		400	
May 13	Sales		540	May 13	Stationery		40	
May 13	Sales	50		May 13	R. Wilkinson			450
				May 13	Stolen money		50	
				May 14	Balance c/d		60	2,130
		800	2,990				800	2,990
May 14	Balance b/d	60	2,130					

Purchases

		£			£
May 2	W. Jones	175	May 14	Trading account	625
May 3	R. Wilkinson	450			
		625			625

W. Jones

		£			£
May 6	Purchases returns	34	May 1	Balance b/d	410
May 6	Bank	410	May 2	Purchases	175
May 14	Balance c/d	141			
		585			585
			May 14	Balance b/d	

Shop fittings

		£			£
May 2	Shopfitters Ltd	1,000	May 14	Balance c/d	1,000
		1,000			1,000
May 14	Balance b/d	1,000			

Shopfitters Ltd

		£			£
May 14	Balance c/d	1,000	May 2	Shop fittings	1,000
		1,000			1,000
			May 14	Balance b/d	1,000

R. Wilkinson

		£				£
May 13	Bank	450	May 3	Purchases		450
		450				450

Purchases returns

		£				£
May 14	Trading a/c	34	May 6	W. Jones		34
		34				34

Sales

		£				£
May 14	Trading a/c	1,290	May 6	Cash		700
			May 13	Bank		540
			May 13	Cash		50
		1,290				1,290

Drawings

		£				£
May 11	Cash	250	May 14	Capital		250
		250				250

Stationery

		£				£
May 13	Cash	40	May 14	Profit and loss a/c		40
		40				40

Capital

		£				£
May 14	Drawings	250	May 1	Balance b/d		31,100
May 14	Balance c/d	30,850				
		31,100				31,100
			May 14	Balance b/d		30,850

Stock

		£				£
May 1	Balance b/d	1,410	May 14	Trading a/c		1,410
		1,410				1,410

Stolen money

		£				£
May 13	Cash	50	May 14	Profit and loss account		50
		50				50

Premises

		£			£
May 1	Balance b/d	28,000	May 14	Balance c/d	28,000
		———			———
		28,000			28,000
May 28	Balance b/d	28,000			

(b) Trial balance of P. Black as at 14 May 1983

	Dr.	Cr.
	£	£
Cash	60	
Bank	2,130	
Purchases	625	
W. Jones		141
Shop fittings	1,000	
Shopfitters Ltd		1,000
Purchases returns		34
Sales		1,290
Stolen money	50	
Stationery	40	
Capital		30,850
Opening stock	1,410	
Premises	28,000	
	£33,315	£33,315

5.6 Further exercises

Question 5.1

The Oran Company keeps very little cash in its office. All cheques and cash received are banked immediately. All payments are made by cheque, except that certain small payments of £20 or less may be made from petty cash. A main cash book is kept with two columns on each side. One column on each side is used to record cash discounts, while the other is used to keep a record of the bank account. Small payments are recorded in a petty-cash book with four analysis columns: postage, travelling, sundry expenses, and small purchases.

(a) From the following information write up the firm's bank cash book and petty-cash book for the week ended 15 December 1982.

December		£
10	Balance at bank	410.27
	Petty cash in hand	7.36
	Vouchers held by petty cashier	92.64
	Petty cashier presented vouchers to main cashier and obtained a refund	
	Postage stamps	10.00
	Banked cheques received from	
	P. Winters (cash discount £2.24)	216.18
	R. Makeson (cash discount £3.16)	317.17
	T. Soames (cash discount £nil)	171.00
11	A member of the company drew foreign currency	100.00
	The bank charged for the service	2.84
12	Director's fare to London	18.60

	13	The following accounts were paid by cheque:	
		Leon Manufacturing Ltd. (cash discount £4.60)	225.40
		Palton Traders Ltd. (cash discount £2.04)	174.16
	14	Window cleaner paid	5.00
		Postage stamps purchased	10.00
	15	Small item of stock purchased for cash	15.81
		Drew cheque for wages	200.00
		P. Winters' cheque returned R/D	
		Errand boy's fare	1.70

(b) A bank statement was received on 17 December 1982 showing a balance at bank of £277.56. From the information given, what may account for the difference between the books and the bank statement?

(c) Why is it necessary to keep a separate column for purchases of stock made from petty cash?

(L)

Answer 5.1

(a)

Cash book

		Discount £	Bank £			Discount £	Bank £
Dec. 10	Balance b/d		410.27	Dec. 10	Petty cash		92.64
Dec. 10	P. Winters	2.24	216.18	Dec. 11	Travel advance		100.00
Dec. 10	R. Makeson	3.16	317.17	Dec. 11	Bank charges		2.84
Dec. 10	T. Soames		171.00	Dec. 13	Leon Manufacturing	4.60	225.40
				Dec. 13	Palton Traders	2.04	174.16
				Dec. 15	Wages		200.00
				Dec. 15	P. Winters		216.18
				Dec. 15	Balance c/d		103.40
		5.40	1,114.62			6.64	1,114.62

Petty-cash book

Receipts £	Date	Details	Total £	Postage £	Travelling £	Sundry £	Purchases £
7.36	Dec. 10	Balance b/d					
92.64	Dec. 10	Bank					
	Dec. 10	Postage	10.00	10.00			
	Dec. 12	Travelling	18.60		18.60		
	Dec. 14	Window cleaning	5.00			5.00	
	Dec. 14	Postage	10.00	10.00			
	Dec. 15	Purchases	15.81				15.81
	Dec. 15	Travelling	1.70		1.70		
			61.11	20.00	20.30	5.00	15.81
	Dec. 15	Balance c/d	38.89				
100.00			100.00				
38.89	Dec. 15	Balance b/d					

(b) Refer to Chapter 6. Difference of £174.16 could represent Palton Traders Ltd cheque unpresented.

(c) Such items representing purchases of goods for resale will be posted to the purchases account and not any other expense account.

Question 5.2

Fred Ogden opened a hardware shop on 1 April 1984. He had £1,000 cash, of which he placed £900 into a bank account. The transactions for the shop during the month of April were:

			£ p
April	3	Purchased goods from T. Duke on credit	150.00
	4	Paid half year's rent by cheque	600.00
	7	Cash sales for week	685.40
		Cash drawings by J. Jones	100.00
		Paid cash into bank	500.00
	8	Purchased goods from B. Prince on credit	75.50
		Purchased goods from R. Knight on credit	115.00
	11	Paid T. Dukes a/c by cheque in full settlement	135.00
	14	Cash sales for week	732.80
		Paid cash into bank	600.00
		Cash drawings by J. Jones	100.00
		Purchases from B. Prince on credit	125.00
	18	Paid B. Prince by cheque	75.50
		Paid R. Knight by cheque, on account	50.00
	19	Sales to J. Lord on credit	30.00
	21	Cash sales for week	483.70
		Paid cash into bank	500.00
	23	Purchases from R. Knight on credit	176.30
	24	Bought cash register from ABC Ltd for credit	172.00
	25	J. Lord settled his account by cheque (less 10 per cent discount)	?
	28	Cash sales for week	572.50
		Paid into bank	700.00
		Drawings by cheque − J. Jones	200.00

Note: Candidates should calculate the amount of the cheque paid by J. Lord on April 25.

From this information you are required to

(a) record the appropriate transactions in a three-column cash book, and bring down the balances as at 30 April 1984;

(b) write up the ledger account of T. Duke, B. Prince and J. Lord and bring down the balances as at 30 April 1984.

Answer 5.2

(a)

Cash book

		Discount £	Cash £	Bank £				Discount £	Cash £	Bank £
April 1	Capital		100.00	900.00	April 4	Rent				600.00
April 7	Sales		685.40		April 7	Drawings			100.00	
April 7	Cash			500.00	April 7	Bank			500.00	
April 14	Sales		732.80		April 11	T. Dukes	15.00			135.00
April 14	Cash			600.00	April 14	Bank			600.00	
April 21	Sales		483.70		April 14	Drawings			100.00	
April 21	Cash			500.00	April 18	B. Prince				75.50
April 25	J. Lord	3.00		27.00	April 18	R. Knight				50.00
April 28	Sales		572.50		April 21	Bank			500.00	
April 28	Cash			700.00	April 28	Bank			700.00	
					April 28	Drawings				200.00
					April 30	Bal c/d			74.40	2,166.50
		3.00	2,574.40	3,227.00			15.00		2,574.40	3,227.00
May 1	Balance b/d		74.40	2,166.50						

(b)

T. Duke

		£			£
April 11	Bank	135.00	April 3	Purchases	150.00
April 11	Discount received	15.00			
		150.00			150.00

B. Prince

		£			£
April 18	Bank	75.50	April 8	Purchases	75.50
April 21	Balance c/d	125.00	April 14	Purchases	125.00
		200.50			200.50
			April 30	Balance b/d	125.00

J. Lord

		£			£
April 19	Sales	30.00	April 25	Bank	27.00
			April 25	Discount allowed	3.00
		30.00			30.00

Question 5.3

(a) For what purposes does a business keep a petty-cash book?   *[3 marks]*

(b) Explain the imprest system of keeping petty cash.   *[4 marks]*

(c) Explain how the petty-cash book would be balanced at the end of the accounting period. Where would the petty-cash book closing balance be shown at the end of the financial year? [3 marks]

(d) Explain what happens to the total of the postage and stationery column. [2 marks]

(e) Explain what happens to the items in the column headed Ledger Accounts. [3 marks]

Answer 5.3

(a) Refer to Section 5.4. To record small payments.
(b) Refer to Section 5.4. Reimbursing amounts paid to restore cash held to agreed float.
(c) Refer to Answer 5.1. Current asset on balance sheet.
(d) Debited to the expense account for postage and stationery.
(e) Debited to the respective ledger accounts.

6 Bank Reconciliation

6.1 Introduction

The cash book of a business shows the balance which the business considers it has as cash at the bank. In the same way as an individual receives a bank statement and compares it with his own records, in whatever form they may be, so a business must make that same comparison. The object of this chapter will be to discover differences between the balance shown on the bank statement and the balance according to the business's own records.

6.2 Types of differences

(a) Error

Errors may be either calculation errors or errors due to failure to record items or recording them twice. Under this heading we also include standing order payments which we have instructed the bank to make but which we have not recorded in our books.

(b) Bank Charges and Interest

Bank charges and interest will be entered by the bank on our account with them, and if we do not make an entry in our books for these amounts, then this will result in a difference.

(c) Timing

When we send a cheque to a supplier, we enter the amount immediately in our cash book. However, allowing time for the supplier to receive the cheque and pay it into his bank account and then for it to find its way to our bank will mean that our account at the bank will not be debited for at least a few days and often much longer. Similarly, there will be a delay, although usually less, from the time we enter cheques received in our cash book to the time they are credited to our account by the bank.

(d) Dishonoured Cheques

When we pay a cheque into our bank account, the bank will credit our account the next day and then proceed to collect the value of that cheque from the bank of our customer who sent us the cheque. If because our customer has insufficient funds in his account or for some other reason the bank will not honour the cheque, then our bank will debit our account with the value of the dishonoured cheque, since it has previously credited our account and is now unable to collect the money.

6.3   Identifying the differences

In comparing the cash book with the bank statement we must remember that cash at bank is an asset to the business and as such we will debit the account to increase the asset and credit it to reduce it. Our bank statement represents our personal account in the books of the bank and therefore the entries will be the opposite to those in our cash book. For example, cheques received from our customers are debited to the bank account in our books but the bank credits our account in their books. To identify differences, we must therefore tick the items appearing as debits in our cash book and credits on our bank statements. Similarly, we can tick items appearing as credits in our cash book and debits on our bank statement.

6.4   Preparing the reconciliation

There are three methods of preparing or writing out the reconciliation:

(i)   Reconcile the bank balance per the bank statement to the cash book balance.
(ii) Reconcile the cash book balance to the bank balance per the bank statement.
(iii) Adjust both balances as appropriate to a corrected balance, which will be the same in both cases — i.e. corrected cash book balance and corrected bank statement balance.

Unless the examination question instructs you to do otherwise you should follow method (iii). Using this method, we must add to our balance in the cash book any receipts not recorded in the cash book or recorded at less than the correct amount. We must deduct from this balance any charges or payments not recorded in our books or recorded at less than the correct amount. This calculation will give us a corrected cash book balance. We must then take the balance per the bank statement and add to it any receipts not recorded on the bank statement. We must then deduct from this any payments which we have made and entered in our cash book but which have not yet been debited to our account at the bank. The amount which we arrive at should then agree with the corrected cash book balance above.

6.5   Worked examples

Example 6.1

Jim Duddy received a statement from his bank at 30 April 1983, showing a balance of £1,420 in his favour. The differences between his cash book and bank statement balances at 30 April are given below.

(1) An amount of £421, paid into bank on 29 April, has not been entered by the bank.

(2) Two cheques drawn by Duddy were not presented for payment until after 30 April: C. Walker £206, P. Higgins £39.

(3) The bank made standing order payments, amounting to £168, on behalf of Duddy. This had not been recorded in the cash book.

(4) On 23 April 1983 Duddy received from V. Bennett a cheque for £306, which he paid to bank on the same day. The bank statement showed that this cheque was dishonoured on 28 April 1983.

(5) On 24 April Duddy paid into bank a cheque for £360, which he received from a customer in full settlement of a debt of £375. This item was shown correctly in the bank statement but Duddy had entered the full £375 in the bank column of his cash book.

(6) J. Ellis, a debtor, had made a payment of £292 direct to the bank but this entry had not been entered in Duddy's cash book.

REQUIRED

(a) A statement showing the corrected bank statement balance.　　　　　　　[4 marks]

(b) The cash book (bank columns only) showing the opening balance at 30 April, the additional entries now made necessary and closing with the corrected balance. [7 marks]

(c) An explanation of why a credit balance on a bank statement represents an asset to the firm concerned.　　　　　　　[4 marks]

(AEB)

Solution 6.1

		£
(a)	Balance as per bank statement	1,420
	add cheques not yet credited (1)	421
		1,841
	less cheques not yet presented (2)	245
	Corrected bank statement balance	1,596

(b)

Cash book

		£			£
April 30	Balance b/d	1,793	April 30	Standing orders (3)	168
April 30	J. Ellis	292	April 23	V. Bennett (4)	306
			April 24	Discount allowed (5)	15
			April 30	Balance c/d	1,596
		2,085			2,085

The cash book adjustments can be explained as follows.
(3) Standing orders not entered.
(4) Since we had previously debited the bank account with £306 and credited V. Bennett's account with £306, we must now reverse that entry.
(5) The original entry would have been a debit to bank account of £375 — i.e. £15 more than the correct figure of £360.

(c) Refer to Section 6.3. Bank statement is personal account of business in bank's books.

6.6 Further exercises

Question 6.1

(a) Do you consider the cash book to be a division of the ledger, a book of original entry, or both? Give reasons for your answer.

(b) A 'Bank Reconciliation Statement' is part of the double-entry system compiled to check the accuracy of the bank statement and the correctness of the firm's own bank records. Comment on this statement.

(c) On 31 December 1982 the balance of cash at bank shown in a firm's cash book was £976.44. A bank statement up to and including 31 December 1982 showed the following:

	£
Bank charges debited to the account	7.94
Credit transfer payments made by customers for which no other notification had been received	247.00
Insurance payment made by standing order not entered in the cash book	25.00
There was no mention in the statement of cheques entered in the cash book and paid to suppliers	219.18

Make the necessary adjustments to the balance shown in the cash book to ascertain the correct amount of cash available — i.e. the amount which should be shown as 'Cash in bank' on a balance sheet dated 31 December 1982.

(L)

Answer 6.1

(a) Refer to Section 7.2.

(b) Incorrect: refer to Section 6.1.

(c) £976.44 add £247.00 less £7.94 less £25.00 — i.e. £1,190.50.

Question 6.2

The cash book kept by Martin Barron showed that he had a balance of cash at the bank at 30 December 1983 of £15,429. On the same date his bank statement showed a balance in hand of £17,520.

On investigation you discover:

(a) a cheque drawn in payment of an account of £571 had been entered in the cash book as £751 and, at 30 December 1983, had not been presented to the bank for payment;

(b) further cheques drawn, amounting to £1,732, had not been presented to the bank for payment at 30 December 1983;

(c) the bank had made a direct debit of £125 on 29 December 1983; there was no entry in the cash book for this item;

(d) bank charges of £86 were charged in the bank statement on 20 December 1983, but no entry had been made in the cash book;

(e) cheques received on 30 December 1983, amounting to £181, had been entered in the cash book and banked immediately, but no entry appeared in the bank statement.

You are asked:

(i) to prepare a statement showing the correct balance in the cash book at 30 December, 1983;

(ii) to prepare a reconciliation statement, reconciling the bank statement balance with the corrected cash book balance at 30 December, 1983.

(SUJB)

Answer 6.2

		£
(i) Balance as per cash book		15,429
add (a) overstatement of payment (£751 − £571)		180
		15,609
less (c) direct debit not entered in cash book	125	
(d) bank charges not entered in cash book	86	211
Corrected cash book balance		£15,398
(ii) Balance per bank statement		17,520
less cheques not yet presented (£1,732 + £571)		2,303
		15,217
add cheques not yet credited		181
		£15,398

Question 6.3

Paul Summerbee reconciled his cash book with the bank statement every month. His bank reconciliation statement for the month of November was as follows:

Balance as per statement 30.11.81.   £4,500.00 overdrawn
Add unpresented cheques:

J. Soap	54.00	
A. Smith	110.00	
M. Pym	26.00	190.00
Balance as per cash book (CR)		£4,690.00

The following is the extract of the bank column in the cash book for the month of December 1981, and a copy of the bank statement for the same month.

1981	Receipts	£		1981	Payments	£
Dec. 1	L. Cleary & Sons	4,180.00	Dec. 1	Balance b/d	4,690.00
4	Lewis & Stanley Ltd.	750.00	5	Perkins Ltd	46.00
5	Ralfs Computers	3,420.00	8	Haynes & Co.	92.00
19	Mullin Printers	221.00	16	Pyper Finance	110.00
23	Higson Ltd.	540.00	23	Hodgson Building Co.	249.00
29	Moore & Co.	399.00	29	Pennington Printers	75.00
			31	Balance c/d	4,248.00
		£9,510.00			£9,510.00

1981		Dr	Cr	Balance	
		£	£	£	
Dec. 1	Balance b/f			4,500.00	O/D
	J. Soap	54.00		4,554.00	O/D
2	L. Cleary & Sons		4,180.00	374.00	O/D
4	Lewis & Stanley Ltd		750.00	376.00	CR
	A. Smith	110.00		266.00	CR

43

5	Regal Insurance Co. – Standing order	65.00		201.00 CR
	Ralfs Computers		3,420.00	3,621.00 CR
8	Perkins Ltd.	46.00		3,575.00 CR
19	Pyper Finance	110.00		3,465.00 CR
	Bank charges	66.00		3,399.00 CR
22	Mullen Printers		221.00	3,620.00 CR
23	Carus Ltd. – Credit transfer		365.00	3,985.00 CR
29	Higson Ltd.		540.00	4,525.00 CR
	Bank commission	45.00		4,480.00 CR
	L. Cleary & Sons – refer to drawer	4,180.00		300.00 CR

From the above information you are required to prepare:

(a) the corrected cash book balance as at 31 December 1981;

(b) a bank reconciliation statement as at 31 December 1981, using the amended cash book balance.

Answer 6.3

		£
(a) Balance per cash book		4,248.00
add received from Carus Ltd (23 Dec.)		365.00
		4,613.00
less		
standing order Regal Insurance (5 Dec.)	65.00	
bank charges (19 Dec.)	66.00	
returned cheque	4,180.00	
bank commission (29 Dec.)	45.00	4,356.00
Corrected cash book balance		£257.00

		£
(b) Bank balance per statement		300.00
add cheque not yet credited Moore and Co. (29 Dec.)		399.00
		£699.00
less cheques not yet presented		
Haynes & Co	92.00	
Hodgson Building	249.00	
Pennington Printers	75.00	
M. Pym	26.00	442.00
Balance per corrected cash book		£257.00

7 Day Books and VAT

7.1 Introduction

So far we have emphasised the importance of the double-entry system of book-keeping. For each transaction which we have looked at we have explained the double entry involved — that is, the debit to one account and the credit to another. This is an important principle, which has to be understood. However, the number of transactions quickly becomes very large in even the smallest of businesses and to record every transaction as a double entry would be unwieldy. In the life of a business there are many transactions of a similar nature — i.e. there will be many credit sale transactions. The purpose of day books is to summarise all of these transactions of a like nature and to make one entry in the ledger for the sum total of all those transactions. These books are also called books of prime entry or books of original entry. They are not part of the double-entry system. We shall now examine these various books.

7.2 Cash book

We mentioned in Chapter 5 that the cash book was a combination of the bank account and the cash account. It is, however, also a day book in that it records daily transactions and is the book of original entry. Unlike other day books, the cash book may be part of the double-entry system, or there may be a separate cash account recording totals in the ledger, in which case the cash book is not part of the double-entry system.

In examination questions, unless they state anything to the contrary, you should assume that cash book means a book of original entry which also acts as part of the double-entry system. Chapter 5 illustrates this type of system.

7.3 Petty-cash book

The uses and advantages of the petty-cash book were discussed in Chapter 5. As with the main cash book, it may or may not be part of the double-entry system.

7.4 Purchases day book

The purchases book records details of all credit purchases of goods for resale. The details are obtained from suppliers' invoices. An example of the purchases day book, or purchases journal, as it may also be called, is shown below.

Date	Supplier	Invoice No.	Goods value	VAT	Invoice value
			£	£	£
Oct. 6	Jones & Co.	1,234	100	15	115
Oct. 7	Express Co.	1,235	1,500	225	1,725

Before we look at the next step we should clarify two items.

(i) Goods value is the amount charged by the supplier before adding VAT (see below) but after deducting any trade discounts. Do not confuse these with cash discounts, referred to in Chapter 5. Trade discounts are allowed to trade customers irrespective of how long they take to pay. Cash discounts are offered for prompt payment.

(ii) Value added tax is charged by suppliers for most types of goods; we shall examine this subject in more detail in Section 7.9.

At the end of each month or such other length of time as the business decides, the latter three columns will be totalled and an entry posted to the ledger as follows:

Dr. Purchases account (with total goods value)
Dr. VAT account (with total VAT charged)
   Cr. Creditors account (with total invoice values)

7.5 Purchases returns day book

We record in the purchases returns day book details from credit notes given to us by suppliers in respect of goods which we have returned to them. The details recorded will be similar to those in the purchases day book. At the end of the period the book will be totalled and an entry made in the ledger as follows:

Dr. Creditors account (with total value of credit notes)
   Cr. VAT account (with VAT on credit notes)
   Cr. Purchases returns account (with goods value as shown on credit notes)

7.6 Sales day book

The sales day book records details of all credit sales by the business. The details are obtained from copy sales invoices. An example of the sales day book, or sales journal, as it is also called, is shown below.

Date	Customer	Invoice No.	Goods value	VAT	Invoice value
			£	£	£
Oct. 6	Greentrees Ltd	1,274	600	90	690
Oct. 7	Bluestars Ltd	1,275	160	24	184

Again we clarify two points before continuing.

(i) Goods value is the amount which we charge our customers before adding VAT (see below) but after deducting trade discounts.

(ii) When we invoice our customers, we will have to charge VAT for most types of goods.

At the end of the period the latter three columns are totalled and an entry made in the ledger as follows:

Dr. Debtors account (with total invoice value)
    Cr. VAT account (with VAT charged to customers)
    Cr. Sales account (with goods value)

7.7   Sales returns day book

We record in the sales returns day book details of all credit notes which we have sent to customers for goods which they have returned to us. The details will be similar to those recorded in the sales day book. At the end of the period the book will be totalled and an entry made in the ledger as follows:

Dr. Sales returns account (with goods value)
Dr. VAT account (with VAT on credit notes)
    Cr. Debtors account (with total credit note value)

7.8   The journal

We should record in the journal all transactions which are not entered into one of the other day books — e.g. purchase on credit of fixed assets; transfers between accounts; correction of errors. We keep the journal in order to have some control over entries in the ledger and also to make it easier to locate any differences which we may discover as a result of taking out a trial balance.

The form of the journal to record the purchase of a motor van on credit from Greenford Autos might be as follows:

		Dr.	Cr.
		£	£
March 30	Motor vehicles	6,600	
	Greenford Autos		6,600
	Being purchase of van on credit from Greenford Autos		

The narration is important for audit and control purposes, and should indicate the reason for the entry and, where appropriate, the authority for it.

7.9   Value added tax

We have already seen that when a business purchases goods and incurs VAT, the VAT amount is debited to a VAT account. When a business charges VAT, this is credited to the VAT account. At the end of each quarter the business sends to H.M. Customs and Excise a remittance for the difference btween VAT charged to customers and the VAT the business has itself suffered on purchases. The amount of this remittance is debited to the VAT account and the bank account is credited. In this way the VAT account acts as a personal account for H.M. Customs and Excise, and any balance on the account at the balance sheet date is shown as a debtor or creditor on the balance sheet, as appropriate.

7.10 Worked examples

Example 7.1

You are required to copy the following table on your answer paper and then to complete the columns. The first item has been completed as an example.

Book of original entry	Details obtained from	Account debited	Account credited
(a) Purchases day book	Invoices received	Purchases	Supplier's
(b) Sales day book			[2 marks]
(c) Purchases returns day book			[2½ marks]
(d) Cash book ('discount received' column)			[2½ marks]
(e) Cash book (sale of the firm's motor van and cheque received in payment)			[2½ marks]
(f) General journal (purchase of fixtures)			[2½ marks]

Solution 7.1

Book of original entry	Details obtained from	Account debited	Account credited
(a)	Invoices received	Purchases	Supplier's
(b)	Copy sales invoices	Customer's	Sales
(c)	Credit notes received	Supplier's	Purchases returns
(d)	Supplier's statement	Supplier's	Discount received
(e)	Credit note received	Bank	Motor van
(f)	Invoice received	Fixtures	Supplier's

Example 7.2

R. Elkins made the following credit purchases on 15 May 1983:

Whitfield Manufacturing Company Ltd
Stock priced at £200 net but subject to 15 per cent VAT

Marketing Company Ltd
Stock at list price £400 subject to a trade discount of 25 per cent and VAT at 15 per cent

Messrs Rook and Crow Ltd
Stock at £300 list price subject to a trade discount of 20 per cent and VAT at 15 per cent
Messrs Rook and Crow Ltd allow a further cash discount of 5 per cent for settlement within 30 days

(a) Set out a purchase day book showing:

    (i) the amount to be credited to the personal account of each supplier;
    (ii) the amount to be debited to the purchases account;
    (iii) the amount to be debited to the VAT account.

(b) The VAT account has been debited with a certain sum of money.

(i) Does this indicate the government is a debtor to R. Elkins?

(ii) How, under normal trading practice, will R. Elkins recover the amounts paid for VAT to suppliers?

(L)

Solution 7.2

(a)

Purchase day book

Date		Goods value (ii) £	VAT (iii) £	Invoice value (i) £
May 15	Whitfield Manufacturing Co. Ltd	200.00	30.00	230.00
May 15	Marketing Co. Ltd	300.00	45.00	345.00
May 15	Rook and Crow Ltd	240.00	36.00	276.00

(i) Credit to supplier's personal account.
(ii) Debit to purchases account.
(iii) Debit to VAT account.

(b)

(i) H.M. Customs and Excise will be a debtor for the amount in (a) (iii).

(ii) R. Elkins will normally recover the amount in (a) (iii) by deducting it from VAT he has charged his customers and collected on behalf of H.M. Customs and Excise.

7.11 Further exercise

Question 7.1

W. Watson is the owner of a small retail outlet. He keeps a full set of accounts, including books of original entry. A selection of his transactions during 1983 is given below.

(1) Purchased goods for resale on credit from D. Crompton £863.
(2) Cash sales £462 (cost price of these goods was £300).
(3) Received £500 from B. Richards (a debtor) on account; paid the full amount into bank.
(4) Bought a motor van, for use in the business, £2,350 on credit from A. Ramsay Motors Ltd. The full debt is repayable before the end of the current accounting period.
(5) Paid the window cleaner, out of petty cash, £5 for cleaning the office windows.

REQUIRED

(a) Completion of the following table for each transaction [(2)–(5) above], naming the book of original entry and the immediate or eventual debit and credit entries. The first one has been done for you as an example. [*6 marks*]

	Book of Original Entry	Debit	Credit
(a) (1)	Purchase day book	Purchases £863	D. Crompton £863

Note: State the amount of money involved in each debit and credit entry.

REQUIRED

(b) Completion of the following table for each transaction [(2)–(5) above], indicating how each transaction would affect gross profit, net profit and working capital. Again, the first one has been done for you, as an example. [*10 marks*]

<table>
<thead>
<tr><th></th><th>Gross Profit</th><th>Net Profit</th><th>Working Capital</th></tr>
</thead>
<tbody>
<tr><td>(b) (1)</td><td>Purchases + £863 but Stock + £863; therefore no effect on gross profit.</td><td>Gross profit no effect: net profit no effect.</td><td>Creditors + £863; therefore current liabilities + £863. Stock + £863; therefore current assets + £863. No effect on working capital</td></tr>
</tbody>
</table>

(AEB)

Answer 7.1

(a)

(2)	Cash book	Cash	Sales
(3)	Cash book	Bank	B. Richards
(4)	Journal	Motor van	A. Ramsay Motors Ltd
(5)	Petty-cash book	Window cleaning	Petty cash

(b)

(2)	Sales + £462 but stock − £300: therefore £162 increase in gross profit	£162 increase, as for gross profit	Cash + £462 but stock − £300; therefore £162 increase in current assets and therefore £162 increase in working capital
(3)	No effect	No effect	Bank + £500 but debtors − £500; therefore no effect on current assets or working capital
(4)	No effect	No effect	Creditors + £2,350; therefore current liabilities + £2,350 and working capital − £2,350
(5)	No effect	Expenses + £5; therefore net profit − £5	Petty cash − £5; therefore current assets − £5 and working capital − £5

8 Errors and Suspense Accounts

8.1 Errors not affecting the trial balance

In Chapter 2 we saw that the purpose of preparing the trial balance was to check the arithmetical accuracy of the books. We also noted that some errors would not be revealed by extracting a trial balance, and we shall now look at those types of error in greater detail.

Errors of omission are errors resulting from the complete failure to enter a transaction in the books.

Errors of commission are errors resulting from the posting of a transaction to the correct type of account but the wrong account: for example, debiting the account of J. Fenner with £100 paid to D. Fenner.

Errors of principle are errors that occur where we debit the wrong type of account: for example, debiting £100 for repairs to buildings to the buildings account (asset) instead of the repairs account (expense).

Compensating errors occur where we make errors which compensate: for example, debiting £150 to the salaries account when the correct figure is £200 and crediting £350 to the sales account when the correct figure is £400.

Reversal of entries occurs where we debit the account which should be credited and credit the account which should be debited.

Errors of original entry occur where the same wrong amount is posted to the debit of one account and the credit of another. Although the accounts to which we enter are correct, the amount is incorrect.

8.2 Correction of errors

(a) Errors of Omission

Errors of omission are corrected by posting the original entry as it should have been posted. For example, we omit to post a payment of £200 through the bank for wages: the correction would be

	Dr.	Cr.
	£	£
Wages account	200	
Bank account		200

(b) Errors of Commission

In order to correct errors of commission, we must cancel out the misposting by an opposite entry to the original and post the item to the correct account. For example, we pay £100 to D. Fenner and debit the account of J. Fenner.

	Dr.	Cr.
	£	£
D. Fenner	100	
J. Fenner		100

(c) Errors of Principle

As with errors of commission, we must cancel out the original entry and post the amount to the correct account. For example, we debit buildings account with £100 paid in respect of repairs to buildings.

	Dr.	Cr.
	£	£
Repairs to buildings account	100	
Buildings account		100

(d) Compensating Errors

We must analyse whether we have debited or credited the account with too much or too little. We then debit the account if either we have previously debited too little or credited too much. We credit the account if either we have originally credited too little or debited too much. For example, to correct an error where we have debited £150 to the salaries account instead of £200 and credited £350 to the sales account instead of £400, the correcting entry would be

	Dr.	Cr.
	£	£
Wages account	50	
Sales account		50

(e) Reversal of Entries

In this case we must reverse our original entry to cancel out that entry and post the transaction as it should have been posted in the first instance. For example, we pay postage of £100 and we debit bank account and credit postage account when, of course, the entry should be the reverse:

	Dr.	Cr.
	£	£
Postage account	100	
Bank account		100
and		
Postage account	100	
Bank account		100

The first entry cancels out and reverses the incorrect entry and the second entry records the transaction as it should have been entered in the books originally.

(f) Errors of Original Entry

If we have posted an amount which is less than the correct amount, we make an additional entry for the amount of the difference, posting to the same accounts as the original entry. If we have posted an amount which is greater than the correct amount, we make an entry for the amount of the difference, posting to the same accounts as the original entry but in reverse — that is, debit where we credited and credit where we debited. This will have the effect of reducing the value of the original entry to its correct amount. For example, we receive £160 from P. Dawson but we debit the bank account with £180 and credit P. Dawson with £180. The correcting entry will be

	Dr.	Cr.
	£	£
P. Dawson	20	
Bank account		20

8.3 Suspense accounts

Suspense accounts are used where a difference arises when we extract our trial balance and we are unable to locate the difference. Of course, every effort should be made to locate the difference and correct the errors, the suspense account being used only as a last resort. Where we need to use a suspense account, we open the account with a balance representing the difference between the two sides of the trial balance. If debit balances are greater than credit balances, then the account is opened with a credit balance, and if credit balances are greater than debit balances, then the suspense account will be opened with a debit balance.

The balance will remain on the suspense account until the error or errors are located, possibly after the final accounts have been prepared. When the errors are discovered, we must correct them, using the suspense account. If we have debited too little to an account or credited too much, then we must debit that account and credit the suspense account. If we have credited too little to an account or debited too much, then we must credit that account and debit the suspense account.

8.4 Worked examples

Example 8.1

P. Wedge is the owner of a small retail outlet dealing in the purchase and sale of golf equipment. On 1 December 1984, the following balances appear in his books:

	£
fittings	620
stock in trade	3,200
motor van	2,500
sales	9,200
returns inward	69
cash at bank	2,600
cash in hand	180
purchases	3,500
drawings	30
trade creditors	2,190
capital	1,479

A trial balance prepared at 1 December 1984, from the above figures, was incorrect owing to:

(1) goods, to the value of £85 (cost price), withdrawn for the personal use of the owner incorrectly credited to the drawings account (the other part of the double entry was correct);

(2) the last physical stock count omitted goods valued at £800;

(3) the complete omission of bank charges £9, levied towards the end of November.

REQUIRED

(a) A corrected trial balance as at 1 December 1984 incorporating the adjustments made necessary by items (1–3) above. Show any such adjustment in brackets next to the relevant item in the trial balance. *[9 marks]*

During the month of December, some of Wedge's transactions were:

(i) purchased goods from a supplier by cheque £1,500;

(ii) purchased goods for resale on credit, £2,300 from P. Green;

(iii) sent a cheque £1,900 to a creditor, S. Iron, for an amount on which 5% cash discount was received;

(iv) sold the motor van (book value £2,000) for £1,800 cash;

(v) returned damaged goods, previously bought on credit, to S. Bunker £93.

REQUIRED

(b) A statement showing which account would be debited and which account would be credited for each of the transactions numbered (i–v) above. The amount involved in each debit and credit entry must be stated and you are advised that some of the transactions may require more than one double entry. *[4 marks]*

(c) Computation of the amount Wedge owed his trade creditors at 31 December 1984. Your answer may be in account form or otherwise but you are advised to show all workings. *[3 marks]*

(d) An explanation of the main purpose of a trial balance. *[1 mark]*

(e) The main reason why Wedge's creditors may offer cash discount terms. *[1 mark]*

(AEB)

Solution 8.1

(a)

P. Wedge Trial Balance as 1 December 1984

	As given Dr.	As given Cr.	Adjustments Dr.	Adjustments Cr.	Corrected Dr.	Corrected Cr.
	£	£	£	£	£	£
Fittings	620				620	
Stock	3,200				3,200	
Motor van	2,500				2,500	
Sales		9,200				9,200
Returns inward	69				69	
Cash at bank	2,600			9(3)	2,591	
Cash in hand	180				180	
Purchases	3,500				3,500	
Drawings	30		85(1)		200	
			85(1)			
Trade creditors		2,190				2,190
Capital		1,479				1,479
General expenses			9(3)		9	
	12,699	12,869			12,869	12,869

54

(1) The correct entry for taking of goods for personal use is

    Dr. Drawings
      Cr. Purchases

The second part of the entry was done correctly, but an adjustment is needed to reverse the original credit to drawings and then to record the transaction correctly.

(2) No adjustment required since it is the closing stock which will be affected. The stock figure appearing in the trial balance will be the opening stock figure.

(3) Dr. General expenses
      Cr. Bank

(b)

	£	£
(i) Dr. Purchases	1,500	
Cr. Cash at bank		1,500
(ii) Dr. Purchases	2,300	
Cr. P. Green		2,300
(iii) Dr. S. Iron	1,900	
Cr. Cash at bank		1,900
Dr. S. Iron	100	
Cr. Discounts received		100
(iv) Dr. Cash in hand	1,800	
Cr. Motor van		1,800
Dr. Loss on disposal	200	
Cr. Motor van		200

(*Note:* This topic is explained in Chapter 11.)

(v) Dr. S. Bunker	93	
Cr. Returns Outward		93

(c)

Creditors

Dec. 31 Cash at bank (Iron)	1,900	Dec. 1 Balance b/d	2,190
Dec. 31 Discounts received (Iron)	100	Dec. 31 Purchases (Green)	2,300
Dec. 31 Returns outward (Bunker)	93		
Dec. 31 Balance c/d	2,397		
	4,490		4,490

(d) Refer to Section 2.2.
(e) Refer to Section 5.2.

Example 8.2

I. Buchanan prepared a trial balance on 31 May 1984, which showed that the total of the credit balances was £350 more than the total of the debit balances. A suspense account was opened with this figure to make the books balance. Later investigations revealed the following errors in his books:

(i) a purchase of £350 was entered wrongly as £200 in the account of the supplier, P. Madoc;
(ii) the purchase by cheque of a piece of office equipment for use in the office, at a cost of £600, had been posted to the purchases account;
(iii) the total of the sales returns book, amounting to £410, had not been posted to the ledger;
(iv) a debit balance on J. Gower's account of £540 was brought down as £450 and this latter figure was included in the debtors' total entered in the trial balance.

You are required to:
(a) prepare the journal entries, including narrations, necessary to correct the above errors;
                                                               [10 marks]
(b) write up the suspense account.
                                                               [5 marks]

Solution 8.2

(a)

(i)

	Dr.	Cr.
	£	£
Suspense account	150	
P. Madoc		150

To credit P. Madoc with £150, being difference between £200 originally entered and correct figure of £350

(ii)

Office equipment account	600	
Purchases account		600

To transfer cost of office furniture originally entered in purchases account

(iii)

Sales returns account	410	
Suspense account		410

Being value of sales returns as per sales returns book not entered in ledger

(iv)

J. Gower	90	
Suspense account		90

To debit J. Gower with difference on balance brought down (£540 less £450)

(b)

Suspense account

	£		£
Balance	350	Sales returns (iii)	410
P. Madoc (i)	150	J. Gower (iv)	90
	500		500

Example 8.3

R. Blackett's trial balance, extracted at 30 April 1982, failed to agree. In early May the following errors were discovered.

1. The total of the returns outward book, £124, had not been posted to the ledger.
2. An invoice received from W. Dawson, £100, had been mislaid. Entries for this transaction had, therefore, not been made.
3. A payment for repairs to the motor van, £36, had been entered in the vehicle repairs account as £30.
4. When balancing the account of R. Race in the ledger, the debit balance had been brought down in error as £26, instead of £62.

REQUIRED

(a) (i) Journal entries, complete with suitable narrations, to correct each of the above errors. [6 marks]
(ii) A suspense account indicating the nature and extent of the original difference in the books. [4 marks]
(iii) The incorrect total of the trial balance credit column, given that the incorrect total of the debit column was £10,000. [2 marks]

REQUIRED

(b) Four types of errors which do not affect the agreement of the trial balance, giving an example of each. [8 marks]

(AEB)

Solution 8.3

(a)

    (i) 1.

	Dr. £	Cr. £
Suspense account	124	
Returns outward account		124

Being value of returns outwards as per returns outwards book not entered in ledger

        2.

Purchases account	100	
W. Dawson		100

Being value of purchases from W. Dawson not posted to ledger
Note: This assumes invoice is for purchases of goods for resale.

        3.

Vehicle repairs	6	
Suspense account		6

Being difference between cost of motor repairs £36 and amount actually posted £30

        4.

R. Race	36	
Suspense account		36

Being error in balance brought down on R. Race's account £62 instead of £26

    (ii)

Suspense account

	£		£
Returns outwards	124	Balance (see note)	82
		Vehicle repairs	6
		R. Race	36
	124		124

Note: This is a balancing figure and therefore assumes that all of the differences have been located.

                                    £

(iii)   Incorrect total of debit column   10,000

Therefore credit column £82 less — i.e. £9,918.

(b)

Refer to Section 8.1; any four from six types described.

8.5   **Further exercises**

Question 8.1   Marks

    (a) State whether each of the following is TRUE or FALSE. In EACH CASE give a reason for your answer.

(i) When you receive your monthly Bank Statement its closing balance should always be the same as the closing balance shown in the Bank Column of your Cash Book.

(ii) The purchase of a Fixed Asset should always be recorded on the DEBIT side of the Profit and Loss account.

(iii) The Bank Account Column in a Cash Book can never have a CREDIT balance.

(iv) Discount Received is transferred at the end of the accounting period to the CREDIT side of the Profit and Loss account   8

(b) What is the purpose of preparing a Trial Balance?   1

(c) Explain THREE DISTINCT types of error NOT disclosed by a Trial Balance. Give an example with each explanation.   6

[15]

Answer 8.1

(a)   (i) False   (ii) False   (iii) False   (iv) True
(b)   Refer to Section 8.1.
(c)   Refer to Section 8.1.

Question 8.2

The trial balance extracted by T. James and Sons, wholesalers, on 30 April 1983 failed to agree and the difference was entered in a Suspense Account. When the books of account were checked later, it was found that the difference had been caused by these errors:

(a) A payment of £470.00 for rates had been entered correctly in the Cash Book but was posted to Rates Account (debit side) as £400.70.

(b) In the F. Mason Account, there were debit entries totalling £1,087.28 and credit entries totalling £1,208.08. The balance was carried down on 30 April 1983 as £110.80 and the amount entered in the trial balance for this account was £110.80 (credit column), as shown in the account.

(c) The total of the Discount Allowed column in the Cash Book had been over-cast by £9.

(d) An entry of £87.50 in the Sales Day Book for goods sold to N. Dailey had not been posted to the N. Dailey Account in the ledger.

(e) The total of Sales Returns Book, £225.90, had not been posted to the ledger.

You are asked:

(1) to prepare journal entries for the correction of these errors;

(2) to make all the necessary entries in the Suspense Account, including the initial entry for the difference in the books.   [18]

(OLE)

Answer 8.2

(1) (a) Dr. Rates	Cr. Suspense	£69.30	
(b) Dr. Suspense	Cr. F. Mason	£10.00	
(c) Dr. Suspense	Cr. Discounts allowed	£9.00	
(d) Dr. N. Dailey	Cr. Suspense	£87.50	
(e) Dr. Sales returns	Cr. Suspense	£225.90	

(2) Suspense account opening balance £363.70 debit

9 Bad Debts and Bad Debts Provision

Examination questions involving bad debts can be centred around the accounting entries to record the writing off of bad debts and the creation, increase and decrease of bad debts provisions. Alternatively, their treatment can be examined as part of a larger question such as a final accounts question. If you can master the principles necessary to answer the first type of question, you should have no difficulty with the second type of question.

9.1 Writing off bad debts

When a debtor is unable to pay his debts and the amount due from him is considered to be irrecoverable, we would not want to leave the balance on his account. To do so would be to carry forward a balance which in reality has no value. The accounting entry is therefore

Dr. Bad debts (an expense account which will be transferred to the profit and loss account)
Cr. A debtor (to reduce/eliminate the amount owing)

If any monies are subsequently received from the debtor, the entry will be

Dr. Cash or Bank
Cr. Bad debts (to reduce the charge to the profit and loss account)

9.2 Making a provision for future bad debts

If we consider that there is a possibility of future bad debts, we do not want to reduce the debtors account, since there is still a chance of recovery of the debt. We do however wish to make a charge against profits in a current accounting period against future bad debts *and* reduce the value of debtors in our balance sheet. The accounting entries are therefore

Dr. Profit and loss account (which will decrease profits)
Cr. Bad debts provision account (the balance on this account being carried forward in the books of account and shown as a deduction from debtors on the balance sheet — thus reducing the value of the debtors)

It is always preferable to maintain a separate bad debts provision account as above. However, it may be that the examination question will require only a bad debts account, in which case the method is identical, as shown in the second worked example.

Once a provision is set up, future bad debts may be either written off direct to a bad debts account or debited to the provision account.

9.3 Adjusting the provision

(a) Accounting Entries

In future periods we may consider our provision to be too large or too small. To increase the provision, we make an accounting entry as in Section 9.2 for the amount of the increase. Conversely, to reduce the provision, we must reverse that entry.

(b) Final Accounts

Faced with a trial balance to which adjustments have to be made from the above, we can make the following rules:

(i) Bad debts – if this appears in the trial balance, write the amount off as a charge in the profit and loss account.
(ii) Bad debts provision – this amount must be deducted from debtors in the balance sheet. If the question requires an adjustment to the provision we must treat any increase as a charge in the profit and loss account, *or* treat any decrease as a credit in the profit and loss account *and* deduct the new provision from debtors in the balance sheet.

9.4 Worked examples

Example 9.1

R. Browling keeps his books on the financial year January to December. The figures below show his debtors at the end of the years indicated.

		£
January to December	1984	8,000
	1985	6,000
	1986	9,000
	1987	9,000

He decided to create a provision for doubtful debts of 5 per cent of debtors in December 1984 and to maintain it at that percentage. Write up the provision for doubtful debts account for the years ended 31 December 1984 to December 1987.

Solution 9.1

Provision for doubtful debts

	£		£
31 Dec. 1984 balance c/d	400	31 Dec. 1984 Profit and loss (1)	400
	400		400
31 Dec. 1985 Profit and loss (2)	100	1 Jan. 1985 balance b/d	400
31 Dec. 1985 balance c/d	300		
	400		400
31 Dec. 1986 balance c/d	450	1 Jan. 1986 balance b/d	300
		31 Jan. 1986 Profit and loss (3)	150
	450		450
31 Dec. 1987 balance c/d	450	1 Jan. 1987 balance b/d	450
	450		450

NOTES

(1) 5 per cent of £8,000   = £400

(2) 5 per cent of £6,000   = £300
     less provision b/f   = £400

     Increase/(decrease) in provision   £(100)

(3) 5 per cent of £9,000   = £450
     less provision b/f   £300

     Increase/(decrease) in provision   £150

Note: No adjustment is required to the provision in 1987, since the level of debtors is unchanged from that in 1986.

Example 9.2

The account shown below was in the ledger of J. Thompson at the end of his accounting year, 31 December 1982, before the final accounts for that year were prepared.

Dr.			Bad Debts Account		Cr.
		£			£
June 5	J. Hanson	218.40	January 1	Provision b/d	170.00
July 22	F. Simpson	112.50	December 15	Cheque (J. Hanson)	21.84
November 6	T. Morrison	96.20			

You are asked:

(a) to prepare the account as it should appear after the preparation of final accounts for the year ended 31 December 1982. Sundry trade debtors at 31 December 1982 totalled £4,100 and the closing provision required is 5% of this amount;

(OLE)

Solution 9.2

Bad debts account

		£			£
June 5	J. Hanson	218.40	Jan. 1	Provision b/d	170.00
July 22	F. Simpson	112.50	Dec. 15	Cheque (J. Hanson)	21.84
Nov. 6	T. Morrison	96.20	Dec. 31	Profit and loss (2)	440.26
Dec. 31	Provision c/d (1)	205.00			
		£632.10			£632.10

NOTES

(1) The year end provision is required to be 5 per cent of £4,100 – i.e. £205.

(2) The figure of £440.26 is the balancing figure required to bring the bad debts provision to the amount calculated in (1) above.

9.5 Further exercise

Question 9.1

D. Davy had an exporting business which adjusted its provision for doubtful debts at the end of the year at a given percentage of the total sundry debtors. The percentage varied each year, depending on the national and international economic situation. Irrecoverable debts were written off during the year to a bad debts account, as and when they were known.

	Bad debts written off during year to bad debts account £	Total debtors at year end £	Rate of percentage for provision of doubtful debts
31 December 1979	750	14,000	5 per cent
31 December 1980	4,085	10,000	10 per cent
31 December 1981	2,900	15,000	5 per cent

From the above information you are required to show:

(a) the bad debts account as affected by the closing entries at the end of the financial years 31 December 1979, 1980 and 1981;

(b) the provision for doubtful debts account for the same years showing the provision brought forward for each year; the balance on this account on 1 January 1979 was £500;

(c) the journal entries for transactions to both the above-named accounts;

(d) an extract from the balance sheets showing how the provision would affect the sundry debtors, as at 31 December 1979, 1980 and 1981.

Answer 9.1

(a)

Bad debts

1979		£	1979		£
Dec. 31	Debtors	750	Dec. 31	Profit and loss	750
1980			1980		
Dec. 31	Debtors	4,085	Dec. 31	Profit and loss	4,085
1981			1981		
Dec. 31	Debtors	2,900	Dec. 31	Profit and loss	2,900

(b)

Provision for doubtful debts

1979		£	1979		£
Dec. 31	Balance c/d	700	Jan. 1	Balance b/d	500
			Dec. 31	Profit and loss	200
		700			700
1980			1980		
Dec. 31	Balance c/d	1,000	Jan. 1	Balance b/d	700
			Dec. 31	Profit and loss	300
		1,000			1,000
1981			1981		
Dec. 31	Profit and loss	250	Jan. 1	Balance b/d	1,000
Dec. 31	Balance c/d	750			
		1,000			1,000
			1982		
			Jan. 1	Balance b/d	750

(c)

	Dr.	Cr.
	£	£
1979 Bad debts	750	
Debtors		750
Being bad debts written off		
1980 as for 1979 but £4,085		
1981 as for 1979 but £2,900		
1979 Provision for doubtful debts		200
Profit and loss	200	
Being adjustment to provision to increase from £500 to £700		
1980 Provision for doubtful debts		300
Profit and loss	300	
Being adjustment to provision to increase from £700 to £1,000		
1981 Provision for doubtful debts	250	
Profit and loss		250
Being adjustment to provision to decrease from £1,000 to £750		

(d)

Balance sheet extracts

	31 Dec. 1979	31 Dec. 1980	31 Dec. 1981
	14,000	10,000	15,000
less provision for doubtful debts	700	1,000	750
	£13,300	£ 9,000	£14,250

10 Control Accounts

10.1 Introduction

We have referred in previous chapters to entries to accounts of debtors and creditors, and this is the area where control accounts are used. We also saw in Chapter 7 how day books reduce the necessity of posting several separate transactions in our ledger. It is the problems associated with a large number of transactions in the ledger that control accounts seek to resolve.

If we consider the problem with a business which has a large number of debtors, we need to have a record of the amounts due from individual debtors in order that we can chase up unpaid debtors for payment. With regard to our final accounts — that is, the balance sheet — we only need a total figure for debtors and this is what control accounts will tell us, since they are nothing more than accounts containing totals. In fact, an alternative name for them is 'total accounts'. The control account contains totals of postings to the individual accounts which it is controlling. For example, a debtors control account or total debtors account contains entries for the total of all items posted to the individual debtor accounts. Similarly, a creditors control account or total creditors account will contain entries for the total of all items posted to the individual creditors accounts.

10.2 Control accounts and double-entry

To give a simple example of control accounts, let us take the following transactions of a new business for the month of January.

Total sales	£10,500
Cash receipts from debtors	£ 9,100

The debtors control account would appear as follows

Debtors control account

		£			£
Jan. 31	Sales	10,500	Jan. 31	Cash	9,100
			Jan. 31	Balance c/d	1,400
		10,500			10,500
Feb. 1	Balance b/d	1,400			

Meanwhile the individual debtors accounts will be debited with the separate sales transactions which make up the £10,500, and individual accounts credited with cash receipts making up £9,100. If this process is followed accurately, at any one time the balances on the individual accounts will total the balance on the control account — in this case £1,400.

At first sight it may appear that we are contravening the rules of double-entry book-keeping, since the transactions are being posted to the individual accounts and the control accounts. That is to say, in the above example we credit sales with £10,500 and debit both the control account and the individual debtors accounts with £10,500. The answer to this apparent inconsistency is that only one of either the control accounts or the individual accounts is part of the double-entry system. Unfortunately for the student, it may be either of these which is part of the double-entry system, but never both. You must read the examination question carefully to ascertain which system is in use. It may be that the control account is part of the double-entry system, in which case the individual accounts will be a subsidiary record. Alternatively, the individual accounts may be part of the double-entry system and the control account will be only a memorandum account.

10.3 Maintaining control accounts

In Section 10.2 we looked at a very simple example of a control account where there were only two types of transactions involved – that is, sales and cash. However, the principle remains the same with all transactions involving the debtors or creditors accounts.

The rule is that the totals of similar transactions posted to the debit of the individual accounts must be posted in total to the control account as a debit. Similarly, the totals of similar transactions posted to the credit of the individual accounts must be posted in total to the credit of the control or total account.

Following this rule we would expect the debit side of the debtors control account to include entries for sales and miscellaneous debits and the credit side to include cash, discounts allowed, sales returns and bad debts. The creditors control account will, on the debit side, include entries for cash, discounts received and purchases returns, while the credit side will include entries for purchases and miscellaneous credits.

10.4 Transferring accounts

Examination questions on control accounts often involve transfers between sales and purchase ledgers. If an account in the sales ledger has a debit balance and is to be transferred to the purchase ledger, we credit the sales ledger control and debit the purchase ledger control. Conversely, a credit balance being transferred from purchase ledger to sales ledger requires an entry debiting sales ledger and crediting purchase ledger.

10.5 Sectionalisation of ledgers

In the larger businesses the sales and/or purchase ledger may be kept in sections – for example, A–J, K–R and S–Z. Exactly the same principles apply with the control account containing entries for the totals of all transactions in the individual accounts which they are controlling.

10.6 Sales and purchases ledgers

These names refer to the ledgers containing the individual accounts for debtors and creditors.

10.7 Worked examples

Example 10.1

R. Pettit's purchase ledger contains the accounts of two creditors with the following balances:

1982		£
August 1	S. Nicholls	260 credit
	G. Price	310 credit

During August the following transactions took place.

1982

August 4   Bought goods from S. Nicholls on credit £624.

August 5   Purchases from G. Price on credit £414.

August 10   Returned damaged goods to S. Nicholls £24.

August 14   Sent S. Nichols a cheque in settlement of his account at 1 August, less 10 per cent cash discount.

August 19   Received a credit note from G. Price for £8 in respect of an overcharge on 5 August.

August 28   S. Nicholls complained that the discount on 14 August should have been 5%. Correct this error.

August 31   G. Price also bought some goods from Pettit. The debit balance of £16 on Price's account in the sales ledger was transferred to his account in the bought ledger.

Pettit had many customers to whom he sold goods on credit. Such debtors totalled £700 on 1 August 1982 and during that month transactions with them were:

	£
Sales	5,300
Returns inward	29
Cheques received	5,356
Discounts allowed	281
Bad debts	35

In addition, the transfer of the balance on the account of G. Price (see 31 August above) was carried out.

REQUIRED

(a) The accounts of Nicholls and Price as they would appear in Pettit's purchase ledger for the month of August 1982.   [8 marks]

(b) The sales ledger control account for the month of August 1982.   [5 marks]

(c) A comment on the purpose of control accounts.   [4 marks]

(AEB)

Solution 10.1

(a)

S. Nicholls

		£				£
Aug. 10	Purchases returns	24	Aug. 1	Balance b/d		260
Aug. 14	Bank	234	Aug. 4	Purchases		624
Aug. 14	Discounts received	26	Aug. 28	Discounts received		13
Aug. 28	Bank (1)	13				
Aug. 31	Balance c/d	600				
		£897				£897
			Sept. 1	Balance c/d		600

G. Price

		£				£
Aug. 19	Purchases (2)	8	Aug. 1	Balance b/d		310
Aug. 31	G. Price (sales ledger) (3)	16	Aug. 4	Purchases		414
Aug. 31	Balance c/d	700				
		724				724
			Sept. 1	Balance c/d		700

NOTES

(1) Represents payment to S. Nicholls of discount deducted in error.
(2) A price reduction should correctly go to purchases account and not purchases returns.
(3) Entry to transfer would be debit G. Price (purchases ledger) and credit G. Price (sales ledger)

(b)

Sales ledger control

		£			£
Aug. 1	Balance b/d	700	Aug. 31	Sales returns	29
Aug. 31	Sales	5,300	Aug. 31	Bank	5,356
			Aug. 31	Discounts allowed	281
			Aug. 31	Bad debts	35
			Aug. 31	G. Price (purchase ledger)	16
			Aug. 31	Balance c/d	283
		6,000			6,000
Sept. 1	Balance b/d	283			

(c)
 (i) An aid to balancing the ledger.
 (ii) Control account under charge of responsible official makes fraud more difficult.
(iii) Total balances readily available.

Example 10.2

Marks

The following information relates to the sales and purchases transactions of
E. MacDon for the month of January, 1983. YOU ARE REQUIRED to select
the appropriate items and draw up:

(i) the Sales Ledger Control Account
and
(ii) the Purchases Ledger Control Account

as they would appear in the General ledger of E. MacDon for January, 1983.

		£
1983		
Jan. 1	Amounts owed by debtors	12,400
Jan. 1	Amounts owed to creditors	3,600

	£
Transactions during January, 1983	
Sales on credit	84,600
Cash sales	19,500
Purchases on credit	43,900
Cash purchases	7,200
Cash received from debtors	81,200
Cash paid to creditors	42,100
Cash discount allowed by suppliers	750
Cash discount allowed to customers	1,250
Credit notes issued for goods returned by customers	250
Credit notes received for goods returned to suppliers	400
Interest charged to debtors on accounts overdue	35
Credit balances on Purchases Ledger accounts transferred to Sales Ledger	100

(SEB)

Solution 10.2

Sales ledger control

		£			£
Jan. 1	Balance b/d	12,400	Jan. 31	Bank	81,200
Jan. 31	Sales	84,600	Jan. 31	Discounts allowed	1,250
Jan. 31	Interest received	35	Jan. 31	Sales returns	250
			Jan. 31	Purchases ledger	100
			Jan. 31	Balance c/d	14,235
		97,035			97,035
Feb. 1	Balance b/d	14,235			

Purchases ledger control

		£			£
Jan. 31	Bank	42,100	Jan. 1	Balance b/d	3,600
Jan. 31	Discounts received	750	Jan. 31	Purchases	43,900
Jan. 31	Purchases returns	400			
Jan. 31	Sales ledger	100			
Jan. 31	Balance c/d	4,150			
		47,500			47,500
			Feb. 1	Balance b/d	4,150

Example 10.3

From the following details prepare the Sales Ledger Control Account and the Purchases Ledger Control Account for the month of March 1983:

	£
Sales Ledger Control Account balance 1 March 1983	7,000
Purchases Ledger Control Account balance 1 March 1983	6,550
Sales	11,000
Purchases	5,450
Receipts from credit customers	10,400
Payments to suppliers for goods on credit	6,300
Returns Inwards	20
Returns Outwards	190
Bad Debts written off	350
Refund of an overpayment made to a credit supplier	60
Discount allowed	130
Transfer of Credit balance from Purchases Ledger to Sales Ledger	100

[*15 marks*]

Solution 10.3

Dr.			Sales ledger control			Cr.
		£				£
Mar. 1	Balance b/d	7,000	Mar. 31	Bank	10,400
Mar. 31	Sales	11,000	Mar. 31	Returns inwards	20
			Mar. 31	Bad debts	350
			Mar. 31	Discounts allowed	130
			Mar. 31	Purchases ledger	100
			Mar. 31	Balance c/d	7,000
		18,000			18,000
April 1	Balance b/d	7,000			

Dr.			Purchases ledger control			Cr.
		£				£
Mar. 31	Bank	6,300	Mar. 1	Balance b/d	6,550
Mar. 31	Returns outwards	190	Mar. 31	Purchases	5,450
Mar. 31	Sales ledger	100	Mar. 31	Bank	60
Mar. 31	Balance c/d	5,470			
		12,060			12,060
			April 1	Balance b/d	5,470

10.8 Further exercises

Question 10.1

The following information refers to the debtors and creditors of **A. M. Suppliers Ltd.**
Balances on 1 December 1984

	£		£
T. Wilkins	380.80	J. M. Barton	490.78
R. Brough	480.35	T. W. Smart	350.85
W. Rilands	107.50		
Total debtors	968.65	Total creditors	841.63

Sales during December 1984			Purchases during December 1984	
Dec.		£	Dec.	£
8	T. Wilkins	170.70	8 J. M. Barton	170.95
10	R. Brough	850.30	12 T. W. Smart	460.05
11	T. W. Smart	110.00		
		1,131.00		631.00

Receipts and payments during December 1984

Dec.		Discount £	Bank £	Dec.		Bank £
4	T. Wilkins	7.60	373.20	3	J. M. Barton	490.78
9	R. Brough		480.35	5	T. W. Smart	350.85
		7.60	853.55			841.63

(a) Open accounts for each customer and supplier together with control accounts for each ledger and post the information given above.

On 31 December it was decided, since T. W. Smart is mainly a supplier, to offset the isolated sale against his account in the purchases ledger.
It was also decided since the W. Rilands account is now long overdue and there appears to be no possibility of receiving payment, to write it off as a bad debt.

(b) Make the entries to record these two decisions.
(c) Balance the accounts and reconcile the two ledgers.

(L)

Answer 10.1

Sales Ledger

T. Wilkins

Dec. 1	Balance b/d	380.80	Dec. 4	Bank	373.20
Dec. 8	Sales	170.70	Dec. 4	Discount	7.60
			Dec. 31	Balance c/d	170.70
		551.50			551.50
Jan. 1	Balance b/d	170.70			

R. Brough

Dec. 1	Balance b/d	480.35	Dec. 9	Bank	480.35
Dec. 10	Sales	850.30	Dec. 31	Balance c/d	850.30
		1,330.65			1,330.65
Jan. 1	Balance b/d	850.30			

W. Rilands

Dec. 1	Balance b/d	107.50	Dec. 31	Bad debts	107.50
		107.50			107.50

T. W. Smart

Dec. 11	Sales	110.00	Dec. 31	Contra Purchases Ledger	110.00
		110.00			110.00

Debtors Control

Dec. 1	Balances b/d	968.65	Dec. 31	Bank	853.55
Dec. 31	Sales	1,131.00	Dec. 31	Discounts	7.60
			Dec. 31	Bad debts	107.50
			Dec. 31	Contra Purchases Ledger	110.00
			Dec. 31	Balances c/d	1,021.00
		2,099.65			2,099.65
Jan. 1	Balances b/d	1,021.00			

Reconciliation:	T. Wilkins	170.70
	R. Brough	850.30
As above		£1,021.00

70

J. M. Barton

Dec. 3	Bank	490.78	Dec. 1	Balance b/d	490.78
Dec. 31	Balance c/d	170.95	Dec. 8	Purchases	170.95
		661.73			661.73
			Jan. 1	Balance b/d	170.95

T. W. Smart

Dec. 31	Contra Sales Ledger	110.00	Dec. 1	Balance b/d	350.85
Dec. 12	Bank	350.85	Dec. 12	Purchases	460.05
Dec. 31	Balance c/d	350.05			
		810.90			810.90
			Jan. 1	Balance b/d	350.05

Creditors Control

Dec. 31	Bank	841.63	Dec. 1	Balances b/d	841.63
Dec. 31	Contra Sales Ledger	110.00	Dec. 31	Purchases	631.00
Dec. 31	Balances c/d	521.00			
		1,472.63			1,472.63
			Jan. 1	Balance b/d	521.00

Reconciliation:	J. M. Barton	170.95
	T. W. Smart	350.05
As above		£521.00

Question 10.2

(a) Explain the term 'suspense account' in connection with the trial balance. Draw up a suspense account showing one entry and explain how it may be cleared. [8 marks]

(b) What is a control account? Give an example of a sales (debtors') ledger control account of a firm which has a large number of customers. Your control account should contain at least four different entries and should be balanced at the period end. [7 marks]

Answer 10.2

(a) Used for difference in trial balance which cannot be located; refer to Section 8.3 and worked examples.

(b) An account which records totals of transactions entered in individual accounts; refer to Section 10.1 and worked examples.

11 Depreciation and Disposal of Assets

11.1 Introduction

In Chapter 4 we defined fixed assets as those held for continuing use in the business. Fixed assets therefore earn profits for a business over several years, which was our reason for showing them on our balance sheet rather than treating them as an expense in our profit and loss account. We must realise, however, that fixed assets do not last forever, except land, although some, such as buildings, may have very long lives. In view of the above, we should make a charge to the profit and loss account each year equal to the part of the cost which we have used. We call this charge depreciation.

11.2 Meaning of depreciation

From the above we could say that depreciation is the spreading of the cost of a fixed asset over its useful life. For example, if a machine costs a business £20,000 and has an expected life of 5 years, it would be reasonable to charge against each year's profits £4,000 (£20,000 ÷ 5).

Although the above is not a strict definition of depreciation, it is satisfactory for us at the moment, and we shall now examine some points for further consideration.

11.3 Total depreciation charge

In Section 11.2 we took the cost of the fixed asset and spread that cost over its expected life. We have therefore ignored the possibility of the asset having a value, albeit a scrap value, at the end of its expected life. If a fixed asset has a value at the end of its life, which we will call its disposal value, then the cost which has to be spread over the life of the asset should be reduced by that disposal value. For example, let us suppose that the fixed asset referred to previously, which cost the business £20,000, has a disposal value after 5 years, its expected useful life, of £2,000. The cost which we now have to spread over 5 years is £18,000 (£20,000 less £2,000) or £3,600 each year.

11.4 The balance sheet value of fixed assets

So far we have indicated that depreciation spreads the cost — that is to say, the amount of the depreciation charge will be an expense to the profit and loss account. Because of this it reduces the amount of our net profit by the amount of that charge, as compared with what the profit would have been if we had not charged depreciation. While this is perfectly true, we must also consider the value at which the fixed asset will be shown in the balance sheet. The balance sheet value of a fixed asset will be its original cost less the sum of all depreciation charges to date. We call this value its net book value.

We shall now show how, on the basis of the figures in Section 11.2 above, the profit and loss account depreciation charge and balance sheet value would be affected. The machine originally cost the business £20,000, and if there were no depreciation charge, that is the value at which it would appear in the balance sheet. However, in year 1 we charge to the profit and loss account a depreciation charge of £3,600 and the balance sheet value will be £16,400 (£20,000 less £3,600). In each of years 2 to 5 we charge £3,600 to our profit and loss account, and our balance sheet values of the fixed asset would be as follows:

at end of year 2	£12,800	(£16,400 less £3,600)
at end of year 3	£9,200	(£12,800 less £3,600)
at end of year 4	£5,600	(£9,200 less £3,600)
at end of year 5	£2,000	(£5,600 less £3,600)

At the end of year 5 we can see that the balance sheet value is equivalent to its estimated disposal value or scrap value.

11.5 Methods of depreciation

There are several methods of calculating the depreciation charge or methods of spreading the cost.

(a) Straight Line Method

The straight line method is the method which we have used in the example above, where the total depreciation charge (that is, cost less residual value) is spread evenly over its expected useful life. With this method the charge for depreciation is the same in each year and is therefore appropriate where each year enjoys equal benefits from the use of the asset.

(b) Reducing Balance Method

The reducing balance method calculates the depreciation charge as a percentage of the net book value at the previous accounting period end. For example, an asset costs a business £20,000 and it is decided to depreciate it at a rate of 40 per cent per annum on the basis of the reducing balance method.

	Depreciation charge for year	Net book value at year end
Year 1	£8,000	£12,000 (£20,000 less £8,000)
Year 2	£4,800 (40 per cent x £12,000)	£ 7,200 (£12,000 less £4,800)
Year 3	£2,880 (40 per cent x £7,200)	£ 4,320 (£7,200 less £2,880)
Year 4	£1,728 (40 per cent x £4,320)	£ 2,592 (£4,320 less £1,728)

We can see that the depreciation charge is substantially higher in the earlier years and can therefore be considered to be appropriate where the business enjoys greater benefit from the asset in its early years because of, for example, greater efficiency. Another argument for the use of this method is in cases where repair and maintenance costs are higher in the later years and these higher costs are then offset by a lower depreciation charge.

From the practical viewpoint, the reducing balance method has the disadvantage that the asset is never fully depreciated. Further, a much higher charge is needed in the early years when compared with the straight line method if the same residual value is to be achieved at the end of its useful life. This method is also referred to as the diminishing balance method.

(c) Machine-hour Method

The machine-hour method, not commonly used, involves taking the total depreciation charge and dividing it by the estimated useful life in hours. The depreciation charge for a period is then calculated by reference to the number of hours that the machine is used in that period. For example, cost of machine is £20,000, residual value £2,000 and estimated life 36,000 hours. If the usage in year 1 were 9,000 hours, depreciation would be calculated as follows:

$$\frac{£18,000 \text{ (total depreciation charge)}}{36,000 \text{ hours (estimated life)}} = £0.50 \text{ per hour}$$

Depreciation charge for year 1 : 9,000 hours at £0.50 = £4,500.

(d) Revaluation Method

The revaluation method is only appropriate for such assets as small tools where there are several small items of low value but nonetheless of lasting value. The depreciation charge is arrived at by comparing the period end valuation of the asset with last period end's valuation as increased by new purchases during the period. For example, at 31 December 1984 a business has loose tools with a value of £400 and purchases new tools during 1985 costing £350. At 31 December 1985 the value of loose tools is £550. Depreciation charge for 1985 would be £200, as follows:

	£
Valuation at 1 January 1985	400
Purchases during 1985	350
	750
less Valuation at 31 December 1985	550
Depreciation charge 1985	£200

11.6 Other factors

We have already stated that the object of depreciation is to write off the cost of the asset (less disposal value) over its expected useful life. We must realise that its balance sheet value will be equal to its cost less amounts of depreciation charged to date. The balance sheet value or net book value does not purport to be the amount for which it could be sold or could be replaced. This is a very important point to realise when looking at the balance sheet of a business.

Another point to be clearly understood is that depreciation has nothing to do with putting aside money to replace an asset. Similarly, we must realise that cash will not necessarily be available to replace that fixed asset. Depreciation writes off the expense of a fixed asset which has already been incurred.

11.7   Accounting entries

We have already seen that the amount of depreciation both creates a charge against profits and reduces the value of the fixed asset in the balance sheet. There are two methods of recording the depreciation, with the same end result.

(a) Method 1

In the first method accounting entries here are

> Dr. Depreciation expense account
> > Cr. Fixed asset account

The balance on the depreciation expense account is transferred at the accounting period end to the profit and loss account.

(b) Method 2

The second method uses a depreciation provision account and the entries are

> Dr. Depreciation expense account
> > Cr. Depreciation provision account

The balance on the depreciation expense account is transferred to the profit and loss account as with method 1, while the balance on the depreciation provision account is deducted from the cost of the fixed asset in the balance sheet. The balance on the depreciation provision account is carried forward to the next account period and is added to each year by repeating the entry above. The net book value of the asset will then be its original cost (as recorded in the fixed asset account) less the balance on the depreciation provision account.

11.8   Fixed asset disposals

When a business sells a fixed asset, there will usually be a profit or loss on disposal. This will be the difference between the sale proceeds and the net book value of the asset. This amount must be debited (if a loss) or credited (if a gain) to the profit and loss account as a gain or loss on disposal of fixed assets. This gain or loss could also be described as a depreciation adjustment, since it reflects an over- or under-charge for depreciation in previous periods.

The accounting entries to deal with the disposal are as follows:

(a) Dr. Fixed asset disposal account
> Cr. Fixed asset account (with the original cost of the fixed asset)

(b) Dr. Fixed asset depreciation provision account
> Cr. Fixed asset disposal account (with the depreciation provided to date on that fixed asset)

The balance on the fixed asset disposal account now represents the net book value of the asset disposed of. If no separate depreciation provision account is maintained, the net book value of the asset should be transferred direct from the fixed asset account to the fixed asset disposal account.

(c) Dr. Bank account

  Cr. Fixed asset disposal account (with the sale proceeds of the fixed asset)

If the asset is disposed of, other than for cash, the personal account of the person acquiring the fixed asset should be debited rather than bank account.

The balance on the fixed asset disposal account now represents the profit or loss or disposal and should be transferred to the profit and loss account.

11.9 Assets purchased/sold during year

When an asset is purchased or sold during the year, we must consider how much depreciation is to be charged for the year during which it is purchased or sold. You must read the examination question carefully to tackle this point, but any of the following may happen:

(a) no depreciation during year of purchase or sale;
(b) one half-year's depreciation in year of purchase or sale;
(c) depreciation calculated pro rata to number of months owned by business (you should assume this method if the question does not tell you otherwise).

11.10 Worked examples

Example 11.1

(a)

Motor Vans Account

1981		£
1 Jan	T. Weldon	30,000

Provision for depreciation

31 Dec.		£
1981	Profit and loss	3,000
1982	Profit and loss	2,700
1983	Profit and loss	2,430
1984	Profit and loss	2,187

The above accounts refer to motor vans purchased. Study the accounts and answer the following questions.

 (i) Were the vans paid for immediately or were they bought on credit?
 (ii) What method of calculation is being used for the depreciation?
(iii) Give the figure of percentage being used for depreciation.
(iv) What is the value of the motor vans shown in the Balance Sheet dated 31 December 1983?

Rewrite the account for the years 1981 and 1982 in the alternative form in which the depreciation appears in the same account as the motor vans. Balance the account at the end of each year.

(b) Hotels often use the revaluation method for calculating depreciation on glass, china, etc. An hotel valued its glass and china at £870 on 1 January 1983, purchased £700 worth during the year and then valued its stock at £1,100 at the end of the year. How much should appear in the hotel's accounts as depreciation for the year ended 31 December 1983?

(c) Name two other items of capital equipment for which the revaluation method of depreciation is most suitable.

(L)

Solution 11.1

(a) (i) Credit, since the account of T. Weldon has been credited.

    (ii) Reducing balance method.

    (iii) 10 per cent $\left(\dfrac{£3{,}000}{30{,}000} \times 100\right)$

    (iv) £19,683 (30,000 − (3,000 + 2,700 + 2,430 + 2,187))

Motor vans account

1981		£	1981		£
Jan. 1	T. Weldon	30,000	Dec. 31	Profit and loss	3,000
			Dec. 31	Balance c/d	27,000
		30,000			30,000
1982			1982		
Jan. 1	Balance b/d	27,000	Dec. 31	Profit and loss	2,700
			Dec. 31	Balance c/d	24,300
		27,000			27,000
1983		£			
Jan. 1	Balance b/d	24,300			

(b)

£470 (as below)

Glass and china

		£			£
Jan. 1	Balance b/d	870	Dec. 31	Profit and loss	470
Dec. 31	Bank	700	Dec. 31	Balance b/d	1,100
		1,570			1,570
Jan. 1	Balance	1,100			

(c) Small tools, jigs, dies.

Example 11.2

Answer each of the following questions:

(a) On 1 January 1978 P. Williams bought a new machine for £3,000. On 31 December 1978 and at the end of every year thereafter 10% of cost was credited to a Provision for Depreciation Account. The machine was sold on 5 January 1982 for £2,000.

Write up a Machine Disposal Account on 5 January 1982 showing clearly the amount to be debited or credited to a Profit and Loss Account to cover the over or under depreciation.

(b) On 1 January 1979 W. Elder bought a new motor van. The van, which cost £4,000, was depreciated every year by 10% of the diminishing balance. The financial year ends on 31 December.

On 2 January 1982 W. Elder sold the van for £2,000.

W. Elder did not keep a separate Provision for Depreciation Account but entered the amount at the end of every year in the van account.

Write up W. Elder's van account for the period 1 January 1979 to 2 January 1982, showing clearly the amount of under or over depreciation to be debited or credited to the profit and loss account.

(c) Outline the revaluation method of calculating depreciation.

On 1 January 1981, W. Beach owned small tools to the value of £4,180.

During the year he purchased new tools at a cost of £427.

On 31 December 1981 he valued his tools at £4,250.

Write up a small tools account showing the amount to be written off to profit and loss.

(L)

Solution 11.2

(a)

Machinery disposal

1982		£	1982		£
Jan. 5	Machinery	3,000	Jan. 5	Depreciation provision (1)	1,500
Jan. 5	Profit and loss (2)	500	Jan. 5	Bank	2,000
		3,500			3,500

NOTES

(1) 5 years at 10 per cent per annum.
(2) Balancing figure.

(b)

Van

1979		£	1979		£
Jan. 1	Bank	4,000	Dec. 31	Profit and loss	400
			Dec. 31	Balance c/d	3,600
		4,000			4,000
1980			1980		
Jan. 1	Balance b/d	3,600	Dec. 31	Profit and loss	360
			Dec. 31	Balance c/d	3,240
		3,600			3,600
1981			1981		
Jan. 1	Balance b/d	3,240	Dec. 31	Profit and loss	324
			Dec. 31	Balance c/d	2,916
		3,240			3,240
1982			1982		
Jan. 1	Balance b/d	2,916	Jan. 2	Bank	2,000
			Jan. 2	Profit and loss (1)	916
		2,916			2,916

NOTE

(1) Balancing figures.

(c) Refer to Section 11.5(d).

Small tools

		£			£
Jan. 1	Balance b/d	4,180	Dec. 31	Profit and loss	357
Dec. 31	Bank	427	Dec. 31	Balance c/d	4,250
		4,607			4,607
Jan. 1	Balance b/d	4,250			

11.11 Further exercises

Question 11.1

(a) Name, and describe briefly, two ways of calculating depreciation and give a numerical example of each.   [*8 marks*]

(b) Explain two ways in which depreciation can be entered into the books of account and the effect of these entries on the balance sheet.   [*7 marks*]

Answer 11.1

(a) (i) Straight line (Section 11.5).
(ii) Reducing balance (Section 11.5).

(b) (i) Use of depreciation provision account (Section 11.7).
(ii) Direct to asset account (Section 11.7).

Question 11.2

1983	PREMISES ACCOUNT		Dr.	Cr.	Balance
Jan. 1	Balance	b/d	20,000		£20,000
April 1	Bank	CB	8,000		£28,000
June 30	Repairs	J	690		£28,690
Nov. 30	Rates	J	2,400		£31,090

EXAMINE the above ledger accounts, then ANSWER THE FOLLOWING QUESTIONS.

	Marks
(a) STATE why the entries for June 30 and Nov. 30 are incorrect.	2
(b) Give the JOURNAL ENTRIES to correct these errors.	4
(c) If the rate of depreciation is set at 25 per cent per annum (using the Fixed Instalment/Straight Line method of calculation), CALCULATE the amount of depreciation for the year ending 31 December 1983.	3
(d) Give the JOURNAL ENTRY to show the depreciation entry in the necessary account. You should assume that a Provision for Depreciation on Premises account is kept.	2

(SEB)

Answer 11.2

(a) (i) June 30   Repairs should be debited to an expense account, not debited to the fixed asset account.
(ii) Nov. 30   Rates should be debited to an expense account, not debited to the fixed asset account.

Neither of the above increases the value of the fixed asset.

(b) (i)

	Dr. £	Cr. £
Building repairs	690	
Premises		690
(ii) Rates	2,400	
Premises		2,400

Note: Add suitable narrations.

(c) 25 per cent × £20,000   = £5,000
25 per cent × £8,000 × $\frac{9}{12}$ = £1,500

Total depreciation expense of £6,500

(d)		Dr.	Cr.
		£	£
Depreciation expense		6,500	
Depreciation provision			6,500
Being depreciation expense for year			

Question 11.3

Stuart Bennet owned a confectioner's retail shop and catering business. The following list of balances was extracted from his books on 31 May 1984:

	£
Purchases	20,000
Sales and catering contracts	50,000
Stock of provisions 1 June 1983	3,300
Debtors (catering contracts)	2,700
Rates	900
Trade creditors	3,600
Provision for doubtful debts	600
Wages	10,200
Motor van expenses for catering contracts	1,000
Light and heating	4,000
Kitchen equipment (cost £6,500)	5,200
Crockery and cutlery	2,100
Motor van (cost £3,000)	2,000
Drawings	5,000
Cash in hand	100
Cash in bank (Dr.)	1,900
Fixtures and fittings (cost £5,000)	3,800
Premises	60,000
Goodwill	20,000
Capital	88,000

From the above balances you are required to prepare a trial balance and a trading and profit and loss account for the year ended 31 May 1984, and a balance sheet as at that date. The following information should be taken into account:

(a) Stock of provisions at 31 May 1984 was £2,800.
(b) Depreciation on fixtures and fittings, the motor van and kitchen equipment is to be calculated at 20 per cent on written-down value, and crockery and cutlery has been revalued at £1,600.
(c) A debtor has been declared bankrupt and £500 is to be written off as a bad debt.
(d) Provision for doubtful debts is to be adjusted to 10 per cent of £2,200.

Answer 11.3
Trial balance

	Dr.	Cr.
	£	£
Purchases	20,000	
Sales		50,000
Stock 1 June 1983	3,300	
Debtors	2,700	
Rates	900	
Trade creditors		3,600
Provision for doubtful debts		600
Wages	10,200	
Motor van	1,000	
Lighting and heating	4,000	

Kitchen equipment	5,200	
Crockery and cutlery	2,100	
Motor van	2,000	
Drawings	5,000	
Cash in hand	100	
Cash at bank	1,900	
Fixtures and fittings	3,800	
Premises	60,000	
Goodwill	20,000	
Capital		88,000
	£142,200	£142,200

Trading profit and loss account of Stuart Bennett for year ended 31 May 1984

			£
Sales			50,000
less Cost of sales (Working 1)			33,640
			16,360
less			
Rates		900	
Bad debts	500		
less Reduction in provision	380	120	
Light and heating		4,000	
Depreciation fixtures and fittings (20 per cent × £3,800)		760	5,780
Net profit			£10,580

Balance sheet of Stuart Bennett at 31 May 1984

		£
Fixed Assets		
Premises		60,000
Fixtures and fittings (£3,800 − £760)		3,040
Kitchen equipment (£5,200 − £1,040)		4,160
Motor vehicles (£2,000 − £400)		1,600
Crockery and cutlery		1,600
Goodwill		20,000
		90,400
Current Assets		
Stock	2,800	
Debtors (Working 2)	1,980	
Cash at bank and in hand	2,000	
	6,780	
less Current Liabilities		
Creditors	3,600	
Working Capital		3,180
Net Assets		£93,580
Capital Employed		
Balance at 1 June 1983	88,000	
add Net profit	10,580	
	98,580	
less Drawings	5,000	
Balance 31 May 1984		£93,580

	£
Stock 1 June 1983	3,300
Purchases	20,000
	23,300
less Stock 31 May 1984	2,800
	20,500
Wages (assumed catering staff)	10,200
Motor van expenses	1,000
Depreciation motor van (20 per cent x £2,000)	400
Depreciation kitchen equipment (20 per cent x £5,200)	1,040
Depreciation crockery and cutlery (£2,100 − £1,600)	500
	£33,640

WORKING 2

Debtors per trial balance	2,700
less bad debt written off	500
	2,200
less provision for doubtful debts	220
	£1,980

Question 11.4

Explain the meaning of the phrase 'depreciation of fixed assets', and indicate THREE methods by which the amount of depreciation for a year can be calculated.

(SUJB)

Answer 11.4

Refer to Sections 11.2, 11.5. Depreciation = spreading the cost, measure of wearing out. Methods: straight line, reducing balance, machine-hour, revaluation.

12 Year End Adjustments

12.1 Introduction

In the examples which we have looked at so far we have considered that the expenses and income which we have entered in our accounts relate exactly to the period for which we are preparing the profit and loss account. For example, if there was a debit of £550 on the rent account, we assumed that that was the rent expense for that accounting period. We shall now consider the accounting treatment where that is not the case and either there is rent owing at the balance sheet date or there is rent paid in advance at the balance sheet date. In both of these cases the amount appearing in our rent account does not represent the true rent expense for that accounting period.

12.2 Accrued expenses

Let us consider the case where a business prepares its profit and loss account to 31 December in each year. The business pays rent two weeks after the end of each quarter in respect of the previous three months. If the business first occupied the premises on 1 January 1985 at a rental of £2,000 per annum, its rent account for 1985 will appear as follows:

		Rent
		£
April 14	Bank	500
July 14	Bank	500
Oct. 14	Bank	500

If we prepared our profit and loss account from the account as it stands, we would show a rent expense of £1,500. This would clearly be incorrect, since the annual rental is £2,000 and we have occupied the premises for the whole year. In order that the correct amount of £2,000 be transferred to the profit and loss account, we need to carry down a credit balance for the amount owing — that is, £500. The rent account would then appear as follows:

			Rent			
1985		£	1985			£
April 14	Bank	500	Dec. 31	Profit and loss account		2,000
July 14	Bank	500				
Oct. 14	Bank	500				
Dec. 14	Balance c/d	500				
		2,000				2,000
			1986			
			Jan. 1	Balance b/d		500

In January 1986, when we pay the rent for the three months ended 31 December 1985, this will appear as a debit on the rent account reducing the balance to nil. This process then continues until the next accounting period end, in this case 31 December 1986, when we examine the situation again to decide whether there is an amount owing.

We have already seen that the balance of £500 on the rent account at 31 December represents the amount owing at that date, and as such it will appear in the balance sheet as an amount owing under current liabilities. The same treatment is applied to any expenses where there is an amount unpaid at the balance sheet date representing expenses actually incurred before that date.

12.3   Prepayments

The opposite situation is where we pay an expense during one accounting period which relates to the next accounting period. Let us consider a situation where the same business as that mentioned in Section 12.2 pays an annual insurance premium on 1 April 1985 of £1,000. If at 31 December we transferred the balance of £1,000 to the profit and loss account, it would not reflect the true expense for the accounting period, since £250 ($\frac{3}{12} \times$ £1,000) relates to the next accounting period. In order that the profit and loss account show the true expense of £750, we need to carry down a debit balance on the account for the £250 prepaid. The insurance account would then appear as follows:

Insurance

1985		£	1985		£
April 1	Bank	1,000	Dec. 31	Profit and loss account	750
			Dec. 31	Balance c/d	250
		1,000			1,000
1986					
Jan. 1	Balance b/d	250			

The balance of £250 brought down into 1986 will then be transferred to the profit and loss account at end of 1986 together with any further expense paid, and after adjusting for any accrual or prepayment at 31 December 1986. In the balance sheet at 31 December 1985 the debit balance of £250 will appear under current assets as a prepayment. The reason for this is that it represents value due to the business at that date.

12.4   Sundry stocks

A year end adjustment should also be made in the case of expenses such as stationery where a stock remains at the year end. The accounting treatment is similar to that for prepayments in that a debit balance is carried down on the expense account, thus decreasing the amount transferred to the profit and loss account. The difference in treatment when compared with prepayments is in the balance sheet treatment of the balance carried down. In the case of sundry stocks it should be shown as such on the balance sheet and not as prepayments.

12.5 Summary

We can summarise the effect on the final accounts of a business of accruals and prepayments as follows. An accrual or amount owing will be added to the amount of the expense which is transferred to the profit and loss account and will also appear under current liabilities as an expense creditor. A prepayment will reduce the amount of an expense transferred to the profit and loss account and will also appear under current assets as a prepayment.

From the above and from Chapter 11, on depreciation, you should notice that all accounting adjustments will affect two items in our final accounts. When we made a depreciation adjustment, we created an expense and reduced the value of the fixed asset. When making any year end adjustments, you should always ensure that two items or accounts are affected. It is often a good idea in examinations to write the names of the two accounts against the adjustment on your examination paper and place a mark against them when you adjust that account. If you do this and you have difficulty in making the balance sheet agree, you can look back to these items to ensure that they are properly ticked.

12.6 Worked examples

Example 12.1

The following balances were extracted from the books of S. Charles, a retail trader, on 30th June, 1982:

	Dr. £	Cr. £
Purchases and Sales	71,400	123,600
Returns Inwards and Outwards	1,600	2,400
Carriage on Purchases	860	
Carriage on Sales	990	
Buildings (at cost price)	100,000	
Furniture and Fittings (at cost price)	10,000	
Provisions for Depreciation		
Buildings		50,000
Furniture and Fittings		2,000
Debtors and Creditors	44,000	9,610
Stock 1st July, 1981	9,400	
Lighting and Heating	5,390	
Office salaries and expenses	10,000	
Discounts allowed and received	620	990
Provision for Doubtful debts		1,200
Insurance	1,100	
Rent and Rates	3,000	
Cash Balance	510	
Bank Balance		2,490
Capital		66,580
	£258,870	£258,870

From the above information and the notes below YOU ARE REQUIRED to prepare a Trading and Profit and Loss account for the year ended 30th June, 1982.
A BALANCE SHEET IS NOT REQUIRED.

FULL WORKING FOR ALL ADJUSTMENTS MUST BE SHOWN AND CLEARLY LABELLED.

NOTES

(1) There were no amounts owing or prepaid at the START of the year on 1 July 1981.

(2) Stock 30 June 1982 . . . £10,300.

(3) Rent and Rates had been paid up to 30 September 1982. There has been no change in the annual amounts charged for Rent and Rates since 1 July 1981.

(4) The following amounts were unpaid at 30 June 1982:
(i) Office expenses . . . £900 (ii) Lighting and Heating . . . £400.

(5) Depreciation is to be calculated as follows:
(i) Buildings at 5 per cent per annum by the STRAIGHT LINE (FIXED INSTAL-MENT) METHOD.
(ii) Furniture and Fittings at 10 per cent per annum by the REDUCING BALANCE METHOD.

(6) Commission payable to salesmen at 1 per cent on Net Sales has not yet been paid.

(7) Provision for Doubtful Debts is to be adjusted to 2½ per cent of Debtors.

(8) Office Expenses included the following items:
(i) Private drawings of £400 by S. Charles.
(ii) Private telephone calls totalling £14 by S. Charles.

(SEB)

Solution 12.1

Trading and profit and loss account of S. Charles for year ended 30 June 1982

			£
Sales			123,600
less returns inwards			1,600
			122,000
less Cost of sales			
Stock 1 July 1981		9,400	
Purchases	71,400		
less returns outwards	2,400		
	69,000		
add carriage on purchases	860	69,860	
		79,260	
less Stock 30 June 1982		10,300	
Cost of sales			68,960
Gross profit			53,040
add Discounts received			990
add Reduction in provision for doubtful debts			100
			54,130
less			
Carriage on sales		990	
Lighting and heating (£5,390 + £400)		5,790	
Office salaries and expenses (£10,000 + £900 − £414)		10,486	
Discounts allowed		620	
Insurance		1,100	
Rent and rates (£3,000 − £750)		2,250	
Depreciation buildings (5 per cent × £100,000)		5,000	
Depreciation furniture and fittings (10 per cent × £8,000)		800	
Commission		1,220	28,256
Net profit			25,874

Note: Although not required by the question, a balance sheet is shown below to complete the illustration.

Balance sheet of S. Charles at 30 June 1982

Fixed Assets	Cost	Depreciation	Net book value
	£	£	£
Buildings	100,000	55,000	45,000
Furniture and fittings	10,000	2,800	7,200
	110,000	57,800	52,200
Current Assets			
Stock		10,300	
Debtors	44,000		
less provision for doubtful debts	1,100	42,900	
Prepayment		750	
Cash		510	
		54,460	
less Current Liabilities			
Creditors	9,610		
Expense creditors (£900 + £400 + £1,220)	2,520		
Bank overdraft	2,490	14,620	
Working capital			39,840
			£92,040
Capital Employed			
Capital balance 1 July 1981		66,580	
add net profit		25,874	
		92,454	
less drawings (£400 + £14)		414	£92,040

Example 12.2

Mr J. Shaw's first year in business as a retailer and general dealer ended on 31 January 1983. He has submitted to you, for checking, his final accounts for the year to 31 January 1983, showing a net profit of £8,170, and his balance sheet as at 31 January 1983.

The balance sheet he had prepared is shown below:

Balance Sheet for first year, ending 31 January 1983

	£		£
Stock	9,150	Trade creditors	10,360
Cash in hand	180	Loan	4,000
Vehicles (cost)	8,300	Capital, 1 February 1982	20,000
Trade debtors	12,210		
Drawings £9,500			
Net profit £8,170	1,330		
Fixtures and fittings (cost)	2,650		
Cash at bank	540		
	34,360		34,360

You agree with his profit calculation and with the amounts shown for the items in the balance sheet, apart from the following:

(a) No depreciation had been included in the profit calculation. Depreciation should have been calculated by the 'straight line' ('equal instalment') method, assuming for the fixtures and fittings a life of 10 years, with no residual value, and for the vehicles a life of 4 years and residual value £700.

(b) The loan was obtained from Superior Finance Co. on 1 October 1982 and interest is payable from that date at the rate of 15 per cent per annum. The loan is to be repaid in full on 30 September 1984. No interest has been paid so far and no entries in respect of the loan interest have been made in the accounts.

(c) Mr Shaw pays the rent of his business premises monthly in advance. The rent for February 1983, £160, was paid in January 1983 and charged by Mr Shaw against the profits of his first year's trading.

(d) Mr Shaw had included his unsold stock in the final accounts and balance sheet at selling price (£9,150). To determine the selling price of his goods, Mr Shaw adds 50 per cent to the cost price.

You are asked:

(1) to calculate the working capital from the balance sheet as it was prepared by Mr Shaw;

(2) to re-calculate the net profit for the first year, showing all your working;

(3) to re-draft the balance sheet, improving the presentation and incorporating any changes needed in view of items (a) to (d) above.

(OLE)

Solution 12.2

(1) Working capital as given. Stock £9,150, add cash £180, add debtors £12,210, add bank £540, less creditors £10,360 = £11,720

(a) no effect	
(b) less interest payable (expense creditor) (15 per cent $\times \frac{4}{12} \times$ £4,000)	200
	11,520
(c) add prepayment	160
	11,680
(d) less reduction in stock valuation (£9,150 $\times \frac{50}{150}$) (1)	3,050
Working capital (revised)	£8,630

NOTE

(1) Cost structure is as follows

Cost price	100
Gross profit	50
Selling price	150

			£
(2) Net profit as given			8,170
(a) less depreciation — fixtures and fittings			
(10 per cent $\times$ £2,650)	265		
— vehicles			
(25 per cent $\times$ £7,600)	1,900		
	2,165		
(b) less interest owing (15 per cent $\times \frac{4}{12} \times$ £4,000)	200		
(c) less reduction closing stock (9,150 $\times \frac{50}{150}$) (1)	3,050		5,415
			2,755
(d) add rent prepaid			160
Net profit (adjusted)			£2,915

NOTE

(1) Reduction in closing stock increases cost of sales, thus decreasing gross profit and, hence, net profit.

(3) Balance sheet of J. Shaw at 31 January 1983

Fixed Assets	Cost	Depreciation	Net book value
	£	£	£
Fixtures and fittings	2,650	265	2,385
Vehicles	8,300	1,900	6,400
	10,950	2,165	8,785

Current Assets
Stock (£9,150 − £3,050)	6,100	
Debtors	12,210	
Prepayments	160	
Cash at bank	540	
Cash in hand	180	
	19,190	

less Current Liabilities
Creditors	10,360	
Interest payable	200	10,560

Working capital	8,630
Net Assets	£17,415

Financed by:
Capital (balance 1 February 1982)	20,000
add Net Profit	2,915
	22,915
less drawings	9,500
Capital (balance 31 January 1983)	13,415
Loan	4,000
	£17,415

Example 12.3

On the last day of his account year, 31 January 1982, three of the accounts in a merchant's ledger were: Stationery Account; Rent and Rates Account; Provision for Depreciation (Office Equipment) Account.

In the Stationery and Rent and Rates Accounts, there are debit entries only, totalling £1,240 (Stationery) and £3,170 (Rent and Rates). Provision for Depreciation (Office Equipment) Account shows a credit balance of £1,830, which had been brought down on 1 February 1981.

At 31 January 1982, £196 is owing for rent, rates have been paid in advance by £140 and the stock of stationery is valued at £325. Further provision for depreciation on office equipment is to be made in respect of the year to 31 January 1982 by the reducing balance method at 20 per cent per annum. The original cost of the firm's office equipment was £3,750.

You are asked:

(a) to open the three ledger accounts with the balances indicated and make all the further entries required in them at year-end;
(b) to show how the balances carried down on these accounts on 31 January 1982 would appear on the Balance Sheet of that date.

(OLE)

Solution 12.3

(a)

Stationery

		£			£
Jan. 31	Balance b/d	1,240	Jan. 31	Balance c/d	325
			Jan. 31	Profit and loss account	915
		1,240			1,240
Feb. 1	Balance b/d	325			

Rent and rates

		£			£
Jan. 31	Balance b/d	3,170	Jan. 31	Balance c/d	140
Jan. 31	Balance c/d	196	Jan. 31	Profit and loss account	3,226
		3,366			3,366
Feb. 1	Balance b/d	140	Feb. 1	Balance b/d	196

Provision for depreciation (office equipment)

1982		£	1981		£
Jan. 31	Balance c/d	2,214	Feb. 1	Balance b/d	1,830
			1982		
			Jan. 31	Profit and loss account (1)	384
		2,214			2,214
			Feb. 1	Balance b/d	2,214

NOTE

(1)   20 per cent × (£3,750 − £1,830) = £384.

(b)

Stationery account − Current assets (stock)	£325
Rent and rates account − Current assets (prepayment)	£140
Current liability (expense creditor)	£196
Provision for depreciation − deduct from office equipment (fixed asset)	

12.7   Further exercises

Question 12.1

(a) Explain, using figures, what is meant by the terms
  (i) accrued expense;
  (ii) prepaid expense. *[4 marks]*
(b) Using your figures from part (a), say how the relevant ledger accounts would be adjusted at period end for accrued and prepaid expenses. *[4 marks]*
(c) Explain the effect and the significance on the balance sheet of accounting for
  (i) accrued expenses;
  (ii) prepaid expenses. *[7 marks]*

(AEB)

Answer 12.1

Refer to Sections 12.2 and 12.3.

Question 12.2

The draft trading and profit and loss account of a business show a profit for the year of £10,320.
On examination, however, the following matters were discovered:

(a) an item of £230 had been omitted from the valuation of the stock-in-trade;
(b) no account had been taken of electricity bills outstanding of £80;
(c) no entry had been made for rates paid in advance amounting to £150;
(d) carriage inwards, amounting to £75, had been credited to the profit and loss account;
(e) depreciation of £630 on plant and machinery had been omitted.

Draw up a statement to show the corrected profits after making adjustments for the above items and indicate the adjustments which will become necessary in the Balance Sheet.

(SUJB)

Answer 12.2

Net profit as calculated		10,320
add (a) increase in closing stock		230
(c) rates prepaid		150
		10,700
less (b) accrued electricity	80	
(d) carriage inwards (2 × £75)	150	
(e) depreciation	630	860
Net profit revised		£9,840

Question 12.3

The following trial balance was extracted from the books of the Sunnyside Holiday Caravan Site on 30 September 1983:

	£ 000	£ 000
Capital, 1 October 1982		175
Rents received for use of sites and vans		140
Vans owned by proprietor of site	25	
Shop sales		70
Shop purchases	45	
Rates	25	
Electricity	7	
Commission received on sale of vans		3
Shop furniture and fittings	10	
Land and buildings	140	
Maintenance tools and equipment	70	
Shop wages	5	
Maintenance wages	25	
Proprietor's cash drawings	7	
Stock taken from shop for proprietor's own use	1	
Insurance	13	
Sundry site expenses	4	
Creditors for shop supplies		2
Cash in hand and at bank	13	
	390	390

Take into account the following:

(i) Of the electricity accounts paid, £5,000 is to be charged to permanent tenants for power used in their vans. The accounts have been sent out but no cash has yet been received. £1,000 is the cost of the general lighting of the site and the remaining £1,000 is the cost of power used in the proprietor's private house.

(ii) £1,000 of the rates paid covers the amount due on the proprietor's house.

(iii) Of the insurance paid, £2,000 is in advance at 30 September 1983.

(iv) All shop stocks are cleared at the end of season.

(v) Depreciation to be charged at the following rates:

Vans	20 per cent of book value
Maintenance tools and equipment	10 per cent of book value
Shop furniture and fittings	10 per cent of book value

Prepare

(a) A shop trading account for the year ended 30 September 1983.

(b) A profit and loss account for the site for the year ended 30 September 1983 and a Balance Sheet on that date.

(L)

Answer 12.3

(a) Shop trading account of Sunnyside Holiday Caravan Site for year ended 30 September 1983

	£000
Sales	70
Purchases	45
Gross profit	25

(b) Profit and loss account of Sunnyside Holiday Caravan Site for year ended 30 September 1983

		£000
Shop net profit (£25,000 − £5,000 − £1,000) (1)		19
Rents received		140
Commission on sale of vans		3
		162
less		
Rates (£25,000 − £1,000)	24	
Electricity (£7,000 − £5,000 − £1,000)	1	
Maintenance wages	25	
Insurance (£13,000 − £2,000)	11	
Sundry site expenses	4	
Depreciation − vans	5	
− maintenance tools	7	77
		£85

NOTE

(1) Shop net profit is gross profit less wages £5,000 and depreciation of shop furniture and fittings £1,000.

Balance sheet of Sunnyside Holiday Caravan Site as at 30 September 1983

Fixed Assets		£ 000
Land and buildings		140
Shop furniture and fittings		9
Maintenance tools and equipment		63
Vans		20
		232
Current Assets		
Prepayments	2	
Tenants (electricity)	5	
Cash in hand and at bank	13	
	20	
less Current Liabilities		
Creditors	2	
Working Capital		18
Net Assets		£250
Financed by:		
Capital (balance 1 October 1982)		175
add net profit		85
		260
less drawings (£7,000 + £1,000 + £1,000 + £1,000) (1)		10
		£250

NOTE

		£000
(1) Drawings	Cash	7
	Electricity	1
	Rates	1
	Stock	1
		£10

Question 12.4

(a) For each of the situations given below, explain
   (i) how each would be entered into the firm's ledger accounts;
   (ii) the effect of each of these entries on the firm's balance sheet:
   (1) **bad debts to be written off**;
   (2) decreasing a provision for bad debts;
   (3) creating a provision for depreciation;
   (4) adjusting a rent receivable account for an amount in arrears at year end. [*12 marks*]

(b) What is the general significance to the firm's balance sheet of adjusting for such items as (1) to (4) above? [*3 marks*]

93

Answer 12.4

(a) (1) (i) dr. bad debts written off a/c, cr. debtors.

(ii) Reduce debtors and net profit; hence, capital.

(2) (i) dr. bad debts provision a/c, cr. profit and loss account.

(ii) Decrease provision for bad debts; hence, increase debtors, increase profit hence capital.

(3) (i) dr. depreciation a/c, cr. fixed asset a/c or depreciation provision account.

(ii) Reduce profits hence capital, reduce value of fixed assets.

(4) (i) Carry down debit balance on rent receivable account.

(ii) Increase profit hence capital, increase debtors.

(b) Refer to Chapters 9, 11 and 12. To show assets at a fair valuation to business and recognise amounts due.

Question 12.5

S. Harrison and Co. keep one account in their Ledger for the rates and insurance on their business premises. Their accounting year runs from 1 July to 30 June.

The local authority's accounting year runs from 1 April to 31 March; rates are demanded in two equal instalments each year. The following payments for rates were made by Harrison and Co.:

28 April 1984, £318.00 (for the period 1 April 1984 to 30 September 1984).

26 October 1984, £318.00 (for the period 1 October 1984 to 31 March 1985).

25 April 1985, £332.00 (for the period 1 April 1985 to 30 September 1985).

The premises were insured for £76,000 (for 1984) and £80,000 (for 1985). The annual insurance premium, calculated at the rate of 15 pence per £100, is payable in advance for the period 1 January to 31 December. The premiums were duly paid by Harrison and Co. on 28 December 1983 (for 1984) and 29 December 1984 (for 1985).

You are asked:

(a) to prepare the Rates and Insurance Account in Harrison and Co.'s Ledger for the year to 30 June 1985;

(b) to say what entries in respect of rates and insurance you would expect to find in Harrison and Co.'s Balance Sheet at 30 June 1985. [*18*]

(OLE)

Answer 12.5

(a)

Rates and insurance account

1984			1985		
July 1	Balance b/d (1)	5,859	June 30	Profit and loss	
Oct. 26	Bank (rates)	318		(balancing figure)	12,343
Dec. 29	Bank (insurance)	12,000	June 30	Balance c/d (2)	6,166
1985					
Apr. 25	Bank (rates)	332			
		18,509			18,509
July 1	Balance b/d	6,166			

WORKINGS

(1) 1 July 1984   prepaid rates   6/12 × £318 =   159
                 prepaid insurance 6/12 × (15% of £76,000)   5,700
                                                                              £5,859

94

(2) 30 June 1985 prepaid rates   6/12 × £332   166
                 prepaid insurance 6/12 × (15% of £80,000)   6,000
                                                                     ───────
                                                                     £6,166
                                                                     ═══════

(b)
        30 June 1985 Balance Sheet extract
            Prepayments   £6,166

13 Departmental Accounts

13.1 Introduction

One of the reasons for keeping accounts is to provide information for the owners and management of the business. One of the important areas of information relates to the profitability of the business. It is obviously important to know the overall or total profit of the business, but in the case of a business running separate departments or selling distinct and separate products it is also useful to know the profit made by each department or earned by each product. This is the purpose of departmental accounts: to provide us with information regarding profitability of separate departments.

We can use this information in various ways. We can compare one department with another with a view to taking action to improve the profitability of the least profitable department. Also, we can ensure that losses within one particular department are not hidden by the overall profit of the business, and, following on from this, we can calculate the effects of closing down any one department.

13.2 Expenses

If we are to calculate the profit of each department, we have to consider how we intend to apportion expenses between departments. There are many and varied bases for doing this, and each business will use bases for apportioning its various expenditures that it considers to be the most logical in the circumstances.

The following list is not exhaustive but will give some ideas of possible bases.

Expense	Basis of apportioning
Rent and rates	Floor area
Canteen costs	Number of employees
Salaries and wages	Time spent in each department
Power, heating and lighting	Actual metered units
Selling expenses	Sales value

13.3 Preparation of departmental accounts

When tackling examination questions on departmental accounts, you should prepare the final accounts in the usual way, as already illustrated, but draw up alongside columns for each department or product. If you complete the total columns first for the whole business, you can then go back and apportion the costs as required to the other columns.

13.4 Worked examples

Example 13.1

D. Bird owns a retail store with two departments, one dealing in electrical goods and the other in furniture. The following information has been extracted from his books for the year ended 31 December 1985:

	£
Premises at cost	26,000
Capital	50,400
Drawings	9,500
Fixtures and fittings at cost	12,000
Motor vehicles at cost	11,000
Provisions for depreciation:	
fixtures and fittings	·4,000
motor vehicles	5,000
Purchases:	
electrical goods	27,950
furniture	50,850
Sales:	
electrical goods	40,000
furniture	80,000
Debtors	4,130
Creditors	5,330
Salaries and wages	21,150
Rates and insurance	1,500
Motor vehicle expenses	3,000
Heating and lighting	2,500
Cash at bank	3,150
Stock (1 January 1985):	
electrical goods	4,200
furniture	7,800

You are required to prepare trading and profit and loss accounts, in columnar form, to show the gross profit and net profit for each department for the year ended 31 December 1985, and a balance sheet for the whole business as at that date, taking into account the following additional information:

(a) Stocks at 31 December 1985 were: Electrical goods £6,400
                                        Furniture £8,700
(b) Fixtures and fittings should be depreciated at 15 per cent on cost and the motor vehicles at 20 per cent on cost.
(c) The floor area occupied by the Electrical Goods Department is 120 square metres and that of the Furniture Department is 180 square metres.
(d) Expenses are to be allocated between the departments on the following basis:
   (i) Rates and insurance and heating and lighting in proportion to the departments' floor areas.
  (ii) Salaries and wages and motor vehicle expenses, other than depreciation, in proportion to the turnover of each department.
 (iii) Depreciation of fixtures and fittings and motor vehicles to be shared equally by the two departments.

Solution 13.1

Trading and profit and loss account of D. Bird for year ended 31 December 1985

	Electrical £		Furniture £		Total £
Sales		40,000		80,000	120,000
Stock (1 January 1985)	4,200		7,800		12,000
Purchases	27,950		50,850		78,800
	32,150		58,650		90,800
less Stock (31 December 1985)	6,400		8,700		15,100
Cost of sales		25,750		49,950	75,700
Gross profit		14,250		30,050	44,300
Salaries and wages	7,050		14,100		21,150
Rates and insurance	600		900		1,500
Motor vehicle expenses	1,000		2,000		3,000
Heating and lighting	1,000		1,500		2,500
Depreciation furniture and fittings	900		900		1,800
Depreciation motor vehicles	1,100	11,650	1,100	20,500	2,200	32,150
Net profit		2,600		9,550	12,150

Balance sheet of D. Bird as at 31 December 1985

Fixed Assets	Cost £	Depreciation £	Net book value £
Premises	26,000		26,000
Fixture and fittings	12,000	5,800	6,200
Motor vehicles	11,000	7,200	3,800
	49,000	13,000	36,000
Current Assets			
Stock		15,100	
Debtors		4,130	
Cash at bank		3,150	
		22,380	
less Current Liabilities			
Creditors		5,330	
Working capital			17,050
Net Assets			£53,050
Capital (balance 1 January 1982)			50,400
add Net Profit			12,150
			62,550
less drawings			9,500
			£53,050

Example 13.2

Adam Parrish carried on a business as a wholesaler selling two distinct products, X and Y. The following information was available on his activities for the year ended 31 March 1981.

Balances as at 1 April 1980	£
Freehold premises at cost	36,000
Capital	118,700
Motor vehicles at cost	20,000
Fixtures and fittings at cost	25,000
Stocks X	6,500
Y	26,000
Provisions for depreciation:	
Motor vehicles	3,500
Fixtures and fittings	4,500

Balances as at 31 March 1981	
Purchases X	35,000
Y	158,000
Sales X	43,500
Y	201,950
Sales returns X	3,500
Y	11,950
Purchase returns X	4,300
Y	14,900
Drawings	9,000
Trade creditors	21,000
Trade debtors	22,950
Balance at bank	18,900
Cash	3,050
Administration expenses	15,000
Selling expenses	21,500

The following further information had not yet been taken into account:

(i) during the year he had taken £450 of good X for his own use; the goods taken were valued at cost price;

(ii) depreciation was to be provided as follows:
motor vehicles 20 per cent on cost
fixtures and fittings 10 per cent on cost;

(iii) stocks at 31 March 1981:

	£
X	7,750
Y	31,200

(iv) commissions owing to sales men as at 31 March 1981 was £1,350;

(v) administration expenses paid for 1981/82 were £1,500.

REQUIRED

(a) Separate trading accounts for each of the products X and Y (columnar presentation may be used) for the year ended 31 March 1981. [10 marks]

(b) A profit and loss account for the whole business for the year ended 31 March 1981. [6 marks]

(c) A detailed statement of the working capital as at 31 March 1981. [6 marks]

(AEB)

Solution 13.2

Trading and profit and loss account of Adam Parrish for year ended 31 March 1981

	X £	Y £	Total £
Sales	43,500	201,950	245,450
less sales returns	3,500	11,950	15,450
	40,000	190,000	230,000

Stock (1 April 1980)	6,500	26,000	32,500
Purchases	35,000	158,000	193,000
less Purchases returns	4,300	14,900	19,200
	30,700	143,100	173,800
	37,200	169,100	206,300
less Stock taken for own use	450		450
	36,750		205,850
less Stock (31 March 1981)	7,750	31,200	38,950
Cost of sales	29,000	137,900	166,900
Gross profit	11,000	52,100	63,100

less

Administration expenses (£15,000 − £1,500)	13,500	
Selling expenses (£21,500 + £1,350)	22,850	
Depreciation motor vehicles (20 per cent × £20,000)	4,000	
Depreciation fixtures and fittings (10 per cent × £25,000)	2,500	42,850
Net profit		20,250

A detailed balance sheet is not required but is shown here for illustrative purposes.

Balance sheet of Adam Parrish at 31 March 1981

Fixed Assets	Cost £	Depreciation £	Net book value £
Premises	36,000	–	36,000
Fixtures and fittings	25,000	7,000	18,000
Motor vehicles	20,000	7,500	12,500
	81,000	14,500	66,500
Current Assets			
Stock		38,950	
Debtors		22,950	
Prepayments		1,500	
Bank balance		18,900	
Cash		3,050	
		85,350	
less Current Liabilities			
Creditors	21,000		
Expenses creditors	1,350	22,350	
Working Capital			63,000
Net Assets			£129,500
Financed by			
Capital (balance 1 April 1980)			118,700
add Net Profit			20,250

less drawings (£9,000 + £450)	138,950	
	9,450	
	£129,500	

13.5 Further exercise

Question 13.1

Fairholm Ltd own a department store with three departments, and the following figures are taken from their books for the year ended 31 December, 1982:

Sales	£
Department A	125,000
Department B	86,000
Department C	75,000

Purchases	
Department A	91,000
Department B	69,000
Department C	55,000

Stock 1 January 1982	
Department A	8,930
Department B	6,110
Department C	6,850

Stock 31 December 1982	
Department A	9,720
Department B	5,870
Department C	6,160

You find that purchases, amounting to £880, have been charged incorrectly to Department C instead of Department B and that sales of £1,350 have been credited to Department A, whereas £750 of this amount should have been credited to Department B and the balance to Department C.

You are asked to prepare:

(a) a trading account for each department after making adjustments for the errors which have been indicated (a columnar form of presentation would be appropriate);

(b) a statement showing the gross profit as a percentage of sales for each department.

(Calculations should be correct to one decimal place.) (SUJB)

Answer 13.1

(a)

Trading account of Fairholm Ltd for the year ended 31 December 1982

		Department				
		A		B		C
		£		£		£
Sales		123,650		86,750		75,600
Stock (1 Jan. 1982)	8,930		6,110		6,850	
Purchases	91,000		69,880		54,120	
	99,930		75,990		60,970	
less Stock (31 Dec. 1982)	9,720		5,870		6,160	
Cost of sales		90,210		70,120		54,810
Gross profit		33,440		16,630		20,790

(b)

	A	B	C
Gross profit margin $\left(\dfrac{\text{Gross profit}}{\text{Sales}} \times 100\right)$	27.0%	19.2%	27.5%

14 Incomplete Records

14.1 Introduction

We have, in previous chapters, looked at the double-entry system of book-keeping. The advantages of the system can be summarised as follows:

(i) There is a complete record of every transaction.
(ii) There is an arithmetical check on the accuracy of the figures.
(iii) Greater control can be exercised over the accounting records.
(iv) Certain subsidiary functions in larger businesses can be delegated to junior staff.
(v) Greater reliability can be placed on the accounts produced from those records.

It would, however, be unrealistic to expect every business to maintain a full set of accounting records using the double-entry system. Many smaller businesses have neither the time nor the experience necessary to do so and can not afford the expense of outside staff to keep such records.

However, every business needs to prepare accounts from time to time, if only to show to the tax authorities, and in this chapter we shall be concerned primarily with the preparation of accounts or at least the calculation of net profit where the double-entry system of book-keeping is not employed. Using the same techniques, we shall also examine how we can prepare accounts, even though rather limited, when accounting records have been lost or destroyed, and we are in the same position as if double-entry accounting records had not been kept. Finally, we might also have to employ the same approach where stock has been physically lost or destroyed and we need to make a calculation of that stock which has been lost or destroyed.

14.2 Statement of affairs

In Section 4.2 we stated that the only time owner's capital is increased or decreased is when profits (or losses) are made or capital is introduced or withdrawn from the business. Taking the worst situation, where there are no records of daily transactions of the business, if we can construct a balance sheet at two dates, then the difference between the two capital balances must be the profit earned by the business, after adjusting for introductions and withdrawals of capital. We cannot, however, construct a balance sheet if we do not have accounts from which to extract balances, but if similar information can be obtained from the owner of the business or elsewhere, we can construct a statement similar to a balance sheet, which we call a statement of affairs. An example may make this clearer.

Dawn Guymer runs a small wholesale business and estimates the assets and liabilities of the business at the following dates to be as stated.

	31 Dec. 1985				31 Dec. 1984		
			£				£
Fixed Assets							
Fittings and equipment			6,000				5,100
Current Assets							
Stock		1,000				1,095	
Debtors		350				490	
Bank		50				50	
Cash		250				5	
		1,650				1,640	
less Current Liabilities							
Creditors	750			770			
Rent owing	60	810	840	80	850	790	
			£6,840				£5,890
Financed by							
Capital (balancing figure)			6,240				5,090
Loans			600				800
			£6,840				£5,890

We can calculate that the capital account has increased by £1,150 (£6,240 − £5,090). If there were no introductions or withdrawals of capital during the year, then her net profit must have been £1,150, subject to the accuracy of the statement of affairs. If fresh capital had been introduced by Dawn Guymer of £500, then her profit would have been £500 less than £1,150 − that is, £650. If, on the other hand, she had withdrawn cash of £1,100 from the business, then her profit would have been £1,100 more than £1,150, making £2,250.

The above profit calculations can be restated by showing the movements in capital as below:

	£		£
Opening capital (1 Jan. 1985)	5,090		5,090
add Capital introduced during year	500	or	–
Net profit (balancing figure)	650		2,250
	6,240		7,340
less Drawings	–		1,100
Closing capital (31 Dec. 1985)	£6,240		£6,240

The above method of calculating profits is unsatisfactory, since it relies on estimates in the statement of affairs and the advantages of double-entry book-keeping listed in Section 14.1 are lost. Additionally, in the case where there are no records of daily transactions such as the above, we have no idea as to how the profit has been earned − for example, the figures for sales, gross profit and expenses.

In cases where we have a detailed record of cash and bank transactions or these can be estimated, we can construct a trading and profit and loss account.

14.3 Trading and profit and loss account from incomplete records

Let us continue the example above, but now the owner is able to supply cash and bank figures from which we construct a cash book as follows:

		Cash £	Bank £			Cash £	Bank £
Jan. 1	Balance b/d	5	50	Dec. 31	Creditors	–	8,010
Dec. 31	Debtors		12,710	Dec. 31	Fittings		900
Dec. 31	Bank	1,545		Dec. 31	Rent		800
				Dec. 31	Other expenses	200	1,255
				Dec. 31	Drawings	1,100	
				Dec. 31	Loan repayment		200
				Dec. 31	Cash		1,545
				Dec. 31	Balance c/d	250	50
		1,550	12,760			1,550	12,760
1986							
Jan. 1	Balance b/d	250	50				

From the above we can calculate sales, purchases and rent by constructing accounts as follows from information in the statement of affairs and the cash book. We can enter the opening and closing balances from the statement of affairs, and the cash and bank figures from our cash book, and we then enter a balancing figure which is the appropriate trading and profit and loss account item. The accounts set out below may help to clarify this.

Debtors

		£			£
Jan. 1	Balance b/d	490	Dec. 31	Bank	12,710
Dec. 31	Sales (balancing figures)	12,570		Balance c/d	350
		13,060			13,060
1986					
Jan. 1	Balance b/d	350			

Creditors

		£			£
Dec. 31	Bank	8,010	Jan. 1	Balance b/d	770
Dec. 31	Balance c/d	750	Dec. 31	Purchases (balancing figure)	7,990
		8,760			8,760
			1986		
			Jan. 1	Balance b/d	750

Rent

		£			£
Dec. 31	Bank	800	Jan. 1	Balance b/d	80
Dec. 31	Balance c/d	60	Dec. 31	Profit and loss account (balancing figures)	780
		860			860
			1986		
			Jan. 1	Balance b/d	60

Alternatively, we can calculate the required figures as follows:

(a) Calculation of sales figure

	£
Amounts received from debtors	12,710
add amounts due from debtors at 31 Dec. 1985	350
	13,060
less amounts due from debtors at 1 Jan 1985	490
Sales for 1985	£12,570

(b) Calculation of purchases figure

	£
Amounts paid to creditors	8,010
add amounts due to creditors at 31 Dec. 1985	750
	8,760
less amounts due to creditors at 1 Jan. 1985	770
Purchases for 1985	£7,990

(c) Calculation of rent expense

	£
Rent paid during year	800
add rent due at 31 Dec. 1985	60
	860
less rent due at 1 Jan. 1985	80
Rent expense for 1985	£780

Using figures from the above accounts, the statement of affairs and cash book, we can now construct a trading and profit and loss account.

Trading and profit and loss account of Dawn Guymer for year ended 31 December 1985

		£
Sales (see debtors account)		12,570
Opening stock (1 Jan. 1985)	1,095	
Purchases (see creditors account)	7,990	
	9,085	
less Closing stock (31 Dec. 1985)	1,000	
Cost of sales		8,085
Gross profit		4,485
less		
Rent (see rent account)	780	
Other expenses (see cash book) (£1,255 + £200)	1,455	2,235
Net profit		£2,250

The net profit of £2,250 agrees with the figure which we arrived at in Section 14.2.

14.4 Goods stolen or lost

If a business loses stock through a burglary or fire, we need to know the value of that stock for insurance purposes. We may be able to find out its value from stock records, but if these do not exist, we may estimate the stock lost if we know our normal gross profit margin. We have so far calculated our gross profit by deducting cost of sales from sales. It is therefore a simple matter if we know gross profit and other trading account items, except closing stock, to insert this latter amount as a balancing figure.

For example, Stuart Davis has a small retail business which suffers a fire on 15 March 1986. He knows that his stock on 1 January was £10,000. His sales since that date have been £30,000, his purchases have been £18,000, and he estimates his gross profit at 20 per cent of sales. We can construct a trading account as follows:

Trading account of Stuart Davis for 11 weeks ended 15 March 1986

		£
Sales		30,000
Opening stock	10,000	
Purchases	18,000	
	28,000	
less Closing stock	4,000(3)	
Cost of Sales		24,000(2)
Gross profit		6,000(1)

NOTES

(1) We know that his gross profit is 20 per cent of sales — that is, £6,000 (20 per cent × £30,000).
(2) Therefore cost of sales is £24,000 (£30,000 less £6,000).
(3) Closing stock must therefore be the difference between cost of goods available for sale of £28,000 and cost of sales £24,000 — that is, £4,000. If, additionally, the business has only incomplete records, it may first be necessary to construct debtors and creditors accounts as in Section 14.3 to find purchases and sales figures.

14.5 Worked examples

Example 14.1

On 31 December 1982 G. Philpott's balances were: premises £55,000; delivery vans £3,900; stock £5,300; bank £4,290; trade debtors £3,910; trade creditors £2,900; capital £69,500. Mr Philpott does not keep full accounting records, but the following information, relating to the half-year ended 30 June 1983, is available.

	£
Cash paid into bank, proceeds of cash sales	24,320
Cheques received from trade debtors	12,900
Cheques drawn for private expenditure	4,500
Cheques drawn for expense items	3,125
Discount allowed	50
Discount received	41
Cheques drawn for payment to suppliers	12,320
Paid for extension to premises by cheque	25,000

A £10,000 bank loan was taken out on 1 April 1983, repayable in equal quarterly instalments over a five-year period with interest at 12 per cent per annum. The first quarterly repayment was made on 30 June with the interest accrued to that date.
Depreciation on delivery vans is at the rate of 20 per cent per annum.
On 30 June 1983 the following figures are available: stock £6,300; trade creditors £1,900; trade debtors £5,300.

REQUIRED

(a) For the six months ended 30 June 1983,
    (i) the bank account;   [*5 marks*]
    (ii) the trade debtors total account and trade creditors total account, showing the calculation of credit sales and credit purchases;   [*5 marks*]
    (iii) the trading and profit and loss accounts;
         NOTE: A balance sheet is NOT required.   [*7 marks*]

(b) An explanation of the purpose of discount allowed and discount received. How does each item affect the proprietor's capital?   [*3 marks*]

                                                    (AEB)

Solution 14.1

(a)
  (i)

Bank

		£			£
Jan. 1	Balance b/d	4,290	June 31	Drawings	4,500
June 30	Sales	24,320	June 31	Expenses	3,125
June 30	Debtors	12,900	June 31	Creditors	12,320
April 1	Loans	10,000	June 31	Premises	25,000
			June 31	Loan	2,500
			June 31	Interest (1)	300
			June 31	Balance c/d	3,765
		51,510			51,510
July 1	Balance b/d	3,765			

NOTE (1)

12 per cent $\times \frac{3}{12} \times$ £10,000 = £300

  (ii)

Debtors

		£			£
Jan. 1	Balance b/d	3,910	June 30	Bank	12,900
June 30	Sales (balancing figure)	14,340	June 30	Discounts allowed	50
			June 30	Balance c/d	5,300
		18,250			18,250
July 1	Balance b/d	5,300			

Creditors

		£			£
June 30	Bank	12,320	Jan. 1	Balance b/d	2,900
June 30	Discounts received	41	June 30	Purchases (balancing figure)	11,361
June 30	Balance c/d	1,900			
		14,261			14,261
			July 1	Balance b/d	1,900

(iii)
Trading and profit and loss account of G. Philpott for 6 months ended 30 June 1983

		£
Sales (£24,320 + £14,340)		38,660
Opening stock (1 Jan. 1983)	5,300	
Purchases	11,361	
	16,661	
less Closing stock (30 June 1983)	6,300	
Cost of sales		10,361
Gross profit		28,299
add Discounts received		41
		28,340
less		
Discounts allowed	50	
Expenses	3,125	
Interest	300	
Depreciation (20 per cent $\times \frac{6}{12} \times$ £3,900)	390	3,865
Net profit		£24,475

A balance sheet, while not required, is shown for illustration purposes.

Balance sheet of G. Philpott as at 30 June 1983

Fixed Assets		£	
Premises		80,000	
Delivery van (£3,900 − £390)		3,510	
		83,510	
Current Assets			
Stock	6,300		
Debtors	5,300		
Bank	3,765		
	15,365		
less Current Liabilities			
Creditors	1,900		
Working Capital		13,465	
		£96,975	
Financed by			
Capital (1 January 1983)		69,500	
add Net Profit		24,475	
		93,975	
less Drawings		4,500	
Capital (30 June 1983)		89,475	
Loan		7,500	
		£96,975	

(b) Discounts allowed to encourage prompt payment from debtors to help cash flow and reduce possibility of bad debts. Expense reduces net profit and therefore capital. Discounts received offered to us by suppliers for same reasons as we offer them to our customers. Income increases profit and therefore owner's capital.

Example 14.2

On 1 January 1981 Colin Jakeman started business buying old motor vehicles, which he broke up, selling good parts as spares and the remainder as scrap metal. All purchases are paid for immediately by cheque and all sales of spares are for cash which is banked immediately. He does not keep a proper set of books, but all transactions are carefully recorded in a note book. The entries for the year ended 31 December 1981 have been summarised as follows:

	£
1 January 1981	
Started business using freehold land and building valued at	70,000
Motor lorry	10,000
Cash in bank	1,000

During the year ended 31 December 1981:	£
Purchases of old vehicles (paid for by cheque)	4,500
Sales of salvaged parts for cash	15,000
Sales of scrap on credit	14,700
Payments received for scrap	13,600
Wages paid to car dismantlers	5,000
Rates paid on property (1 Jan. 1981–31 March 1982)	900
Insurance paid (including £200 for 1982)	1,200
Heating and lighting paid during year	750
Heating and lighting unpaid but due for year ended 31 Dec. 1981	210
Drawings during year	6,000

On 1 July 1981 he purchased a car crushing machine for £30,000. The whole amount was lent to him by the bank. On 31 December the bank debited his current account with a half-year's interest at the rate of 20 per cent per annum and his first repayment of £5,000.

Colin Jakeman agrees that the lorry should be depreciated by 20 per cent of the value at 1 January 1981, and that the crusher should be depreciated by 10 per cent at cost.

On 31 December 1981 stocks of old vehicles, spares, etc., were valued at £500.

A bank statement provided up to and including 31 December 1981 showed a bank balance of £3,550, but cheque stubs revealed that cheques to the value of £300 had not been presented.

Prepare a trading and profit and loss account for the year ended 31 December 1981 and a balance sheet on the date.

(L)

Solution 14.2

Trading and profit and loss account of Colin Jakeman for year ended 31 December 1981

	£	£
Sales (£15,000 + £14,700)		29,700
Purchases	4,500	
less Stock (31 December 1981)	500	
	4,000	
Wages	5,000	
Cost of sales		9.000
Gross profit		20,700
less		

Rates (£900 − £180)	720	
Insurance (£1,200 − £200)	1,000	
Heating and lighting (£750 + £210)	960	
Interest ($20\% \times \frac{6}{12} \times £30,000$)	3,000	
Depreciation motor lorry	2,000	
Depreciation machine	3,000	10,680
Net profit		10,020

Balance sheet of Colin Jakeman as at 31 December 1981

		£
Fixed Assets		
Land and building		70,000
Machine		27,000
Motor lorry		8,000
		105,000
Current Assets		
Stock	500	
Debtors (£14,700 − £13,600)	1,100	
Prepayments (£200 + £180)	380	
Bank (£3,550 − £300)	3,250	
	5,230	
less Current Liabilities		
Expense creditors	210	
Working Capital		5,020
Assets Employed		110,020
Financed by		
Capital (1 January 1981)		81,000
add net profit		10,020
		91,020
less drawings		6,000
Capital (31 December 1981)		85,020
Loan (£30,000 − £5,000)		25,000
		£110,020

Example 14.3

On 1 April 1982, the first day of his accounting year, Mr F. Morris valued the stock in his retail store at £4,570 (cost price).

To determine the selling price of all goods sold, he adds 50 per cent to the cost price.

A fire occurred on 5 November 1982 and the stocktaking immediately afterwards showed the stock remaining after the fire, valued at the lower of cost or market price, to be worth £2,220.

The information below relates to the period from 1 April 1982 to the time of the fire:

	£
Sales	63,840
Purchases	44,540
Returns inwards (all in good condition)	240
Returns outwards	540
Stock drawings by Mr Morris for his own use (cost price)	680

Mr Morris made a claim on his insurance company and eventually accepted £2,750 in full settlement.

You are asked to show your calculation (which can be partly or wholly in the form of an account, if you wish) of the net loss sustained by Mr Morris through the fire.   [5]

(OLE)

Solution 14.3

Trading account of F. Morris for period 1 April 1982 to 5 November 1982 (assuming no fire)

	£	£
Sales		63,600
Opening stock (1 April 1982)	4,570	
Purchases (£44,540 less £540)	44,000	
	48,570	
less stock taken for own use	680	
	47,890	
less Closing stock (balancing figure) (2)	5,490	
Cost of sales (1)		42,400
Gross profit ($\frac{50}{150} \times$ £63,600)		£21,200

NOTES

(1) Sales less gross profit.
(2) £47,890 − £42,400

	£
Stock immediately before fire (as above)	5,490
Stock undamaged in fire	2,220
Stock damaged in fire	3,270
Insurance settlement	2,750
Net loss sustained by F. Morris	£520

14.6 Further exercises

Question 14.1

On 1 May 1982, A. Jackson opened a photographic studio and paid £14,000 into a business bank account as the commencing capital.

He kept no proper books of account for his first year in business, but the summary given below, covering the year to 30 April 1983, has been prepared from statements supplied by the bank.

	£
(a) Payments into the business bank account:	
Capital, 1 May 1982	14,000
Payments received for photographic work done (after deducting A. Jackson's	
drawings and certain expenses − see below)	9,554
(b) Cheques drawn on the business bank account:	
Purchase of equipment (furniture and fittings, cameras, dark-room equipment, etc.)	11,220
Advertising	265
Lighting and heating	656

Rent, rates and insurance		3,490
Miscellaneous expenses		214
Payments to suppliers of photographic materials		2,730

Mr Jackson tells you that the total amount received by him for photographic work done was £19,560. He explains that the difference between this total and the amount paid into bank is accounted for by: drawings £8,100, wages of a part-time assistant £1,840, miscellaneous expenses £66.

You are asked to prepare a Profit and Loss Account for the year ended 30 April 1983 and a Balance Sheet as at 30 April 1983, taking the following matters into consideration:

 (i) Unpaid bills from suppliers of photographic materials totalled £525 at 30 April 1983.
(ii) £950 is to be allowed for depreciation of equipment.
(iii) At 30 April 1983, the stock of photographic materials is valued at £620.
(iv) The item above for rent, rates and insurance (£3,490) includes the premium paid (£144) on an insurance policy covering a 12 months' period starting on 1 August 1982.
(v) Mr Jackson tells you that at 30 April 1983 £2,720 is owing to him for work done. He estimates, however, that only three-quarters of this amount will be collected eventually.

[20]

(OLE)

Answer 14.1

Profit and loss account of P. Jackson for year ended 30 April 1983

		£
		£
Sales (£19,560 + £2,720)		22,280
Purchases of materials (£2,730 + £525)	3,255	
less Stock of materials (30 April 1983)	620	
		2,635
		19,645
less		
Advertising	265	
Lighting and heating	656	
Rent, rates and insurance (£3,490 − ($\frac{3}{12}$ × 144))	3,454	
Miscellaneous expenses (£214 + £66)	280	
Wages	1,840	
Depreciation of equipment	950	
Provision for doubtful debts (25% × £2,720)	680	8,125
Net profit		£11,520

Balance sheet of A. Jackson as at 30 April 1983

			£
Fixed Assets			
Equipment (£11,220 − £950)			10,270
Current Assets			
Stock		620	
Debtors	2,720		
less provision for doubtful debts	680	2,040	
Prepayments		36	
Bank		4,979	
		7,675	
less Current Liabilities			
Creditors		525	
Working Capital			7,150
Net Assets			17,420

Financed by

Capital (1 May 1982)		14,000
add net profit		11,520
		25,520
less drawings		8,100
Capital (30 April 1983)		17,420

Question 14.2

A. Dawson, a property repairer, does not keep his business accounts by double-entry but it has been ascertained that the assets and liabilities on 1 September 1984 were:

	£
Equipment	4,600
Bank overdraft	2,284
Sundry debtors for work done	3,900
Vehicles	5,200
Trade creditors (for materials purchased)	2,280
Cash in hand	200
Stock of materials	2,450

The entries made in the business Cash Book for the year ended 31 August 1985 have been summarised as follows:

	£
Payments made to suppliers of materials	9,870
Vehicle running expenses	856
Assistant's wages	4,460
Amount received for work carried out	28,570
A. Dawson's drawings	6,240
Miscellaneous expenses	852
Purchase of equipment	1,600

At 31 August 1985:

(a) after allowing for depreciation, the 31 August 1985 Balance Sheet figures for equipment and vehicles were: equipment £5,200, vehicles £3,800;

(b) stock of materials was valued at £2,860;

(c) £4,100 was owing by customers for work done;

(d) cash in hand was £200;

(e) £2,580 was owing to creditors for materials purchased.

You are asked:

(1) to calculate the capital of A. Dawson's business at 1 September 1984;

(2) to show your calculation, in account form or otherwise, of the bank balance at 31 August 1985;

(3) to prepare suitable final accounts showing the net profit for the year ended 31 August 1985;

(4) to prepare the Balance Sheet at 31 August 1985.

[24]

(OLE)

Answer 14.2

(1)

Statement of affairs of A. Dawson at 1 September 1984

Assets	£
Equipment	4,600
Vehicles	5,200
Debtors	3,900
Stock	2,450
Cash	200
	16,350

less Liabilities

Creditors	2,280	
Bank overdraft	2,284	4,564

Net worth of business (hence, capital) £11,786

(2)

Bank account

1985			1984		
Aug. 31	Debtors	28,570	Sept. 1	Balance b/d	2,284
			1985		
			Aug. 31	Creditors	9,870
			Aug. 31	Vehicle expenses	856
			Aug. 31	Wages	4,460
			Aug. 31	Drawings	6,240
			Aug. 31	Expenses	852
			Aug. 31	Equipment	1,600
			Aug. 31	Balance c/d	2,408
		28,570			28,570
Sept. 1	Balance b/d	2,408			

(*Note:* It is assumed that all of the transactions mentioned in the question have been done through the bank and that the cash in hand remains static at £200.)

(3)

A. Dawson Profit and Loss account for the year ended 31 August 1985

	£	
Revenue from repair work (1)		28,770
Opening stock of materials	2,450	
Purchases of materials (2)	10,170	
	12,620	
less Closing stock of materials	2,860	
Cost of materials used	9,760	
Vehicle expenses	856	
Assistant's wages	4,460	
Miscellaneous expenses	852	
Depreciation equipment (3)	1,000	
Depreciation vehicles (4)	1,400	
Total costs		18,328
Net profit		10,442

WORKINGS

(1) Cash received from customers	28,570
add amounts owing at 31 August 1985	4,100
	32,670
less amounts owing at 1 September 1984	3,900
	28,770
(2) Cash paid to suppliers	9,870
add amounts owing to suppliers at 31 August 1985	2,580
	12,450
less amounts owing to suppliers at 1 September 1984	2,280
	10,170
(3) Equipment value at 1 September 1984	4,600
Purchases during year	1,600
	6,200

less Equipment value at 31 August 1985	5,200
Depreciation for year	1,000
(4) Vehicles value at 1 September 1984	5,200
less Vehicles value at 31 August 1985	3,800
	1,400

(4) A. Dawson Balance Sheet at 31 August 1985

			£
Fixed Assets			
Equipment			5,200
Vehicles			3,800
			9,000
Current Assets			
Stock		2,860	
Debtors		4,100	
Cash at bank		2,408	
Cash in hand		200	
		9,568	
less Current Liabilities			
Creditors		2,580	
Working capital			6,988
			£15,988
Capital			
Balance at 1 September 1984		11,786	
add Net profit		10,442	
		22,228	
less Drawings		6,240	
Balance at 31 August 1985			£15,988

Question 14.3

On 1 January 1980, the total assets of J. McMahon's business were £76,360 and the total liabilities amounted to £29,150. The corresponding figures for 31 December 1980 were: assets £85,740, liabilities £34,290. McMahon's drawings in 1980 amounted to £19,200.

On 31 December 1981, total liabilities were £45,670. Net profit for 1981 was £14,920 and McMahon's drawings in 1981 amounted to £17,500.

On 31 December 1982, total assets were £90,460 and total liabilities were £55,280. The business made a net loss of £1,860 in 1982.

In the period 1 January 1980 to 31 December 1982, no new capital was introduced into the business by J. McMahon.

You are asked to prepare:

(1) statements showing (a) the net profit (or net loss) for 1980, (b) the total assets at 31 December 1981, (c) McMahon's drawings in 1982;
(2) Capital Account for the period 1 January 1980 to 31 December 1982.   [*18*]

(OLE)

Answer 14.3

	1979 £	1980 £	1981 £	1982 £
Assets	76,360	85,740	94,540 (b)	90,460
Liabilities	29,150	34,290	45,670	55,280
Capital	47,210	51,450	48,870	35,180
Capital (opening)		47,210	51,450	48,870
add Net profit (loss)		23,440(a)	14,920	(1,860)
		70,650	66,370	47,010
less drawings		19,200	17,500	11,830 (c)
Capital (closing)		51,450	48,870	35,180

NOTES

(a) (b) and (c) calculated by balancing figures after figures given in question entered in above statement.

15 Income and Expenditure Accounts

15.1 Introduction

An income and expenditure account is prepared for non-trading organisations such as clubs and societies in place of the profit and loss account which we prepare for trading organisations. Items of income and expenditure are shown on this account on the basis of expenses incurred and revenue earned, which means that we must adjust for accruals and prepayments in exactly the same way as we do for trading organisations in the profit and loss account.

Since the object of non-trading organisations is usually not to make a profit but to cover expenses, we use the word 'surplus' rather than profit to refer to the excess of income over expenditure. The opposite of surplus is a deficit.

15.2 Accumulated fund

Non-trading organisations do not usually have a share capital as such, the finance being provided by excesses of income over expenditures. These surpluses are referred to as accumulated fund and described as such in the balance sheet.

15.3 Members' subscriptions

The income and expenditure account needs to reflect subscriptions in respect of the current period only, which means adjusting for accruals and prepayments as follows:

(i) We must exclude any subscriptions paid in advance and relating to the next period. These will form part of the next period's subscription income.
(ii) We must include any subscriptions which are in arrears at the end of the accounting period in so far as they relate to the current period. In the next accounting period we must be sure to exclude those subscriptions, since we have already accounted for them.

An example should help to clarify the adjustments which we need to make.

The Bootle Squash Club receives subscriptions in 1984 amounting to £6,223, of which £57 relates to 1985. At 31 December 1984 £53 is owing to the club in respect of 1984 subscriptions.

	£
Subscriptions received	6,223
add subscriptions in arrears	53
	6,276
less subscriptions paid in advance	57
Income from subscriptions to be shown in accounts	£6,219

£53 in arrears will appear as a debtor in the club's balance sheet and £57 as a creditor.

If in 1985 the club receives subscriptions amounting to £7,010 (including 1984 arrears) and at 31 December 1985 there are subscriptions paid in advance of £41 and subscriptions due unpaid of £93, its subscription income for 1985 would be calculated as follows:

		£
Subscriptions received		7,010
less subscriptions in arrears at 1 Jan. 1985	53	
subscriptions paid in advance (i.e. re 1986)	41	94
		6,916
add subscriptions paid in advance at 1 Jan. 1985	57	
subscriptions in arrears at 31 Dec. 1985	93	150
Income from subscriptions to be shown in accounts		£7,066

Note: It is irrelevant that the full £53 may not have been received and therefore included in the £7,010. We accrued £53 in 1984 and we must therefore reverse that accrual in 1985. We must accept that 1984 accounts have been completed and finalised and cannot be altered.

We can also calculate our subscription income by preparing the subscription account as it would appear in the ledger. Prepayments represents a creditor to the business and therefore a credit balance. Arrears represents a debtor and therefore a debit balance. Subscriptions actually received would be debited to the bank account and credited to the subscriptions account. The balancing figure is the amount transferred to the income and expenditure account. Shown below is the subscription account as it would appear in the books of the Bootle Squash Club.

Subscriptions

1984		£	1984		£
Dec. 31	Balance b/d	57	Dec. 31	Bank	6,223
Dec. 31	Income and expenditure account	6,219	Dec. 31	Balance c/d	53
		6,276			6,276
1985			1985		
Jan. 1	Balance b/d	53	Jan. 1	Balance b/d	57
Dec. 31	Income and expenditure account	7,066	Dec. 31	Bank	7,010
Dec. 31	Balance c/d	41	Dec. 31	Balance c/d	93
		7,160			7,160
1986			1986		
Jan. 1	Balance b/d	93	Jan. 1	Balance b/d	41

15.4 Bar trading account

In order to calculate the bar profit, we normally prepare a bar trading account in the same way as we prepare trading accounts for trading organisations. The bar profit is then transferred to the income and expenditure account. A trading account can be prepared similarly for any subsidiary trading activity carried on by the organisation.

15.5 Other club activities

Other club activities can be dealt with by way of a separate trading account as above. Alternatively, similar items can be netted off on the face of the balance sheet. For example, the cost of raffle prizes can be shown as a deduction from the amounts received from raffle ticket sales, to show a net profit on the raffle.

15.6 Receipts and payments account

We must distinguish the receipts and payments account from an income and expenditure account. The receipt and payments account is a record only of amounts actually received and paid, the balance representing our bank and cash balances. It does not recognise accruals and prepayments but often it will be the document from which we prepare an income and expenditure account, adjusting for accruals and prepayments.

15.7 Worked examples

Example 15.1

The assets and liabilities of the Parkside Cricket Club at 30 September 1981 were:

premises £250,000; subscriptions in arrears £48; equipment £3,200; bank £1,896; bar stocks £920; subscriptions in advance £29; creditors for bar supplies £340; accumulated fund £255,695.

Receipts and payments for the year ended 30 September 1982 were:

Receipts — subscriptions £694 (including £42 owing from last year); bar takings £7,200; socials and dances £320; sub-letting of cricket ground £200;

Payments — equipment £1,000; ground maintenance £1,260; rates £1,200; creditors for bar supplies £2,980; light and heat £220; insurance £86; general expenses £104.

At the end of September 1982, the following further information was available.

1. Subscriptions not received from year ended 30 September 1981 are to be written off.
2. Depreciate equipment by £200.
3. Creditors for bar supplies £786.
4. Subscriptions in arrears £45.
5. Light and heat owing £30.
6. Insurance prepaid £14.
7. Bar stocks £821.

REQUIRED

(a) For the year ended 30 September 1982:
    (i) an account showing the profit or loss on the bar;   *[5 marks]*
    (ii) the income and expenditure account   *[10 marks]*
   Note: A balance sheet is not required.
(b) A statement of the main difference between a non-commercial organisation and a busi-

ness firm. How is this difference reflected in their respective final accounts? [*5 marks*]
(AEB)

Solution 15.1

(a) (i)
Bar trading account for year ended 30 September 1982

		£
Bar takings		7,200
Stock (1 Oct. 1981)	920	
Purchases (1)	3,426	
	4,346	
less Stock (31 Sept. 1982)	821	
Cost of sales		3,525
Bar profits		£3,675

NOTE

(1) Payments £2,980 add creditors (31 Sept. 1982) £786 less creditors (1 Oct. 1981) £340 = £3,426.

(ii)
Income and expenditure account of Parkside Cricket Club for year ended 30 September 1982

	£		£
Ground maintenance	1,260	Bar profit	3,675
Rates	1,200	Subscriptions (1)	720
Light and heat (£220 + £30)	250	Socials and dances	320
Insurance (£86 − £14)	72	Sub-letting	200
General expenses	104		
Depreciation equipment	200		
Surplus income over expenditure	1,829		
	4,915		4,915

NOTE (1)

Dr.			Subscriptions			Cr.
1981		£	1981			£
Oct. 1	Balance b/d	48	Oct. 1	Balance b/d		29
1982			1982			
Sept. 30	Income and expenditure account	720	Sept. 30	Bank		694
				Balance c/d		45
		768				768
Oct. 1	Balance b/d	45				

While not required by the question, a balance sheet is shown for illustrative purposes.

Balance sheet of Parkside Cricket Club at 30 September 1982

Fixed Assets		£
Premises		250,000
Equipment (£3,200 + £1,000 − £200)		4,000
		254,000

Current Assets

Bar stock		821	
Subscriptions in arrears		45	
Prepayments		14	
Bank		3,460	
		4,340	

less Current Liabilities

Bar creditors	786		
Expense creditors	30	816	3,524

Net Assets	£257,524
Accumulated fund at 1 Oct. 1981	255,695
add Surplus for year	1,829
Accumulated fund at 31 Sept. 1982	£257,524

(b)   Refer to text.

Example 15.2

The Balance Sheet of the Compendium Club on 31 December 1982 showed the following:

	£
Subscriptions paid in advance	310
Subscriptions in arrear	24
Bar stocks at cost	540
Bar creditors	173
Balance at bank and cash in hand (including funds held on behalf of charities)	1,437
Furniture and fittings	3,110

The treasurer records receipts and payments in a columnar cash book. The totals of the various columns for the year ended 31 December 1983 are as follows:

	£
Subscriptions	5,110
Bar sales	5,716
Sales of dance tickets	2,176
Dance expenses	749
Rent and rates of premises	2,200
Lighting and heating	1,420
Barman's wages	2,500
Steward's salary	5,000
Collections made on behalf of charities	2,650
Distributions to outside charities	2,600
Purchase of new furniture	1,460
Sale of old furniture (book value £270)	150
Payments for bar purchases	2,610

Take into consideration the following on 31 December 1983:

	£
(i) Subscriptions in arrear	40
(ii) Subscriptions in advance	410
(iii) Bar stocks at cost	470
(iv) Bar creditors	190
(v) Rent unpaid	200
(vi) Depreciation of furniture at 5 per cent of book value on 31 December 1983.	

(a) Prepare a Receipts and Payments Account for the year ended 31 December 1983.

(b) Prepare an Income and Expenditure Account for the year ended 31 December 1983. This account should show clearly the profit or loss on the various activities.

Note: A Balance Sheet is not required. (L)

Solution 15.2

(a)

Receipts and payments account of Compendium Club for year ended 31 December 1982

	£		£
Opening balance b/d	1,437	Dance expenses	749
Subscriptions	5,110	Rent and rates	2,200
Bar sales	5,716	Lighting and heating	1,420
Sale of dance tickets	2,176	Barman's wages	2,500
Collections on behalf of charities	2,650	Steward's salary	5,000
Sale of furniture	150	Distributions to charities	2,600
Closing balance c/d	1,300	New furniture	1,460
		Bar purchases	2,610
	£18,539		£18,539
		Closing balance b/d	1,300

(b)

Income and expenditure account of Compendium Club for year ended 31 December 1982

Dr. Cr.

	£			£
Loss on sale of furniture	120	Bar sales		5,716
Rent and rates (£2,200 + £200)	2,400	Opening stock	540	
Lighting and heating	1,420	Purchases (1)	2,627	
			3,167	
Steward's salary	5,000	less Closing stock	470	
Depreciation furniture (5 per cent × £4,300)	215		2,697	
		add Barman's wages	2,500	5,197
		Bar profit		519
		Dance tickets	2,176	
		less expenses	749	1,427
		Subscriptions (2)		5,026
		Deficit — excess expenditure over income		2,183
	£9,155			£9,155

NOTES

(1) Payments £2,610 add creditors (31 Dec. 1983) £190 less creditors (31 December 1982) £173 = £2,627

(2)

Subscriptions

		£			£
Jan. 1	Balance b/d	24	Jan. 1	Balance b/d	310
Dec. 31	Income and expenditure account	5,026	Dec. 31	Bank	5,110
	Balance c/d	410		Balance c/d	40
		5,460			5,460
1983			1983		
Jan. 1	Balance b/d	40	Jan. 1	Balance b/d	410

Example 15.3

The following information relates to the affairs of Clydeville Social Club, which ended its financial year on 31 December 1983:

		£
1 January 1983	Subscriptions for 1982 in arrear	120
During 1983	Subscriptions for current year received	4,710
	Arrears for 1982 received	90
	Subscriptions paid in advance for 1984	27
31 December 1983	Subscriptions for 1983 not received	84
1 January 1983	Rates in arrears	200
8 January 1983	Rates due in November 1982 paid	400
8 May 1983	Rates due and paid	450
7 November 1983	Rates due and paid	450

Rates due in November each year covers the period from 1 October that year to 31 March in the following year.

Calculate for the year ended 31 December 1983 the amount for (i) subscriptions and (ii) rates which should be shown in the

(a) Receipts and Payments Account,
(b) Income and Expenditure Account,
(c) Balance Sheet at 31 December 1983, as an asset or liability.

(L)

Solution 15.3

(i)

			£
Subscriptions received during 1983	(current year)		4,710
	(1982)		90
	(1984)		27
(a) Receipts and payments account			4,827
less subscriptions in arrears (1 Jan. 1983)		120	
subscriptions paid in advance (re 1984)		27	147
			4,680
add subscriptions in arrears at 31 Dec. 1983			84
(b) Income and expenditure account (1)			4,764

NOTE

(1) This assumes £30 arrears for 1982 is to be written off. Alternative is for arrears at 31 Dec. 1983 to be increased to £114, making amount at (b) £4,794.

(ii)

			£
Rates paid 8 Jan.			400
8 May			450
7 Nov.			450
(a) Receipts and payments account			1,300
less arrears at 1 January		200	
prepayments at 31 December		225	425

(b) Income and expenditure account   £875

(c) Balance sheet 31 Dec. 1983

Assets	£
Subscriptions in arrears	84
Rates prepaid	225
Liabilities	
Subscriptions paid in advance	27

15.8 Further exercises

Question 15.1

The sixth form committee at Camden Square Secondary School run a tuck shop throughout the year with the object of providing funds to pay for a disco for staff and sixth formers at the end of the summer term.

On 1 September 1982, the sixth form took over, from the previous accounting period, a cash balance £25, creditors £15 and stock £8. A summary of the cash account for the ten months ended 30 June 1983 is given below.

Cash Account

Balance b/d	25	Purchases	253
Raffle proceeds	52	Creditors	420
Sales	873	Raffle prizes	8
Building Society interest	4	Raffle tickets	3
		Cost of collecting goods from suppliers	12
		Refreshments	6
		Building Society deposit	100
		Balance c/d	152
	954		954

At 30 June 1983, creditors were owed £42 and IOUs totalling £12 (for goods sold) were discovered in the cash box. There was no closing stock.

REQUIRED

(a) For the 10 months ended 30 June 1983,

    (i) a total creditors account showing the calculation of credit purchases;   *[3 marks]*
    (ii) a trading account to show gross profit on sales;   *[4 marks]*
    (iii) an income and expenditure account incorporating the gross profit made by the tuck shop.   *[4 marks]*

(b) A balance sheet as at 30 June 1983.   *[5 marks]*

The end of year disco was held on 5 July 1983, at a total cost of £242. Sixty staff and one hundred sixth formers attended. Staff were given free admission but sixth formers had to pay an admission fee.

REQUIRED

(c) Assuming creditors were paid in full, all IOUs were received and all funds generated by sixth form activities were utilised, what fee would need to have been charged to each sixth former for admission to the disco?   *[2 marks]*

(d) Assuming selling price of goods was determined by adding 25 per cent to cost (including carriage), explain why you may be dissatisfied with the gross profit figure you have calculated. Give two possible reasons for any discrepancy.   *[2 marks]*

(AEB)

Answer 15.1

(a)   (i)

Creditors

1983		£	1982		£
June 30	Bank	420	Sept. 1	Balance b/d	15
June 30	Balance c/d	42	June 30	Trading account	447
		462			462
			July 1	Balance b/d	42

(ii)

Trading account of tuck shop for 10 months ended 30 June 1983

		£
Sales (£873 + £12)		885
Stock (1 Sept. 1982)	8	
Purchases (£253 + £447)	700	
add collection costs	12	712
Cost of sales		720
Gross profit		£165

(iii)

Income and expenditure account of tuck shop for 10 months ended 30 June 1983

	£			£
Refreshments	6	Gross profit		165
Surplus – excess income over expenditure	204	Raffle proceeds	52	
		less tickets	3	
		prizes	8	11
		Profit on raffles		41
		Interest received		4
	210			210

(b)

Balance sheet of tuck shop as at 30 June 1983

	£
Current Assets	
Debtors	12
Building Society	100
Bank	152
	264
less Current Liabilities	
Creditors	42
Net Assets	222
Financed by	
Fund balance at 1 Sept. 1982 (£25 + £8 − £15)	18
add Surplus 1982/1983	204
Fund balance at 30 June 1983	£222

(c)

Cost of disco

Cost of disco	242
Fund at 30 June 1983	222
Deficit	£20

Each student would need to have been charged 20p (£20 ÷ 100).

(d)
Cost of sales   £720
Therefore anticipated sales £900 (720 + 25 per cent). Sales are £15 less than would have been anticipated. This could be due to
 (i) misappropriation of stock;
 (ii) misappropriation of cash takings;
 (iii) sale of stock at less than the correct prices.

Question 15.2

Wentworth Cricket Club had the following assets and liabilities at 1 January 1984:

	£
ground and pavilion	250,000
equipment	2,300
fixtures and fittings	3,900
subscriptions in arrears (from 1983)	92
subscriptions received in advance (for 1984)	106
light and heat owing	81
insurance prepaid	209
bar stocks	943
members' long term (interest free) loans	50,000
accumulated fund	210,549

Wentworth Cricket Club
Receipts and Payments account for year ending
31 December 1984

	£		£
Balance b/d	3,292	Bar purchases	7,306
Subscriptions	809	Equipment	860
Bar sales	10,243	Lottery tickets and prizes	821
Sales of monthly lottery tickets	4,391	Ground maintenance	4,202
Net proceeds from fruit machines	5,002	Light and heat	320
Loans from members	5,000	Insurance	609
		Extension to pavilion	11,500
		Affiliation fees	30
		Balance c/d	3,089
	28,737		28,737

At 31 December 1984, the following matters were outstanding:
 (1) subscriptions in arrears (for 1984) £23 and subscriptions received in advance (for 1985) £86;
 (2) subscriptions still outstanding for 1983 £22 were to be written off;
 (3) equipment, including additions, had depreciated by 10%;
 (4) insurance prepaid £220 and light and heat owing £90;
 (5) bar stocks at 31 December 1984 was valued at £1,100.

REQUIRED
 (a) An income and expenditure account of the Wentworth Cricket Club for the year ended 31 December 1984. [15 marks]
Note. As a balance sheet is NOT required, you will not need to use **all** of the items given above.
 (b) An explanation of the difference, in accounting treatment at year end, between: (i) subscriptions in arrears and light and heat owing, and; (ii) subscriptions in advance and insurance prepaid. [5 marks]

(AEB)

Answer 15.2

(a)

Wentworth Cricket Club Income and Expenditure account for year ended 31 December 1984

	£		£
Ground maintenance	4,202	Bar profit (1)	3,094
Light and heat (£320 + £90 – £81)	329	Subscriptions (2)	760
Insurance (£609 – £220 + £209)	598	Lottery surplus (£4,391 – £821)	3,570
Affiliation fees	30	Proceeds fruit machines	5,002
Depreciation (10% × £3,160)	316		
Surplus income over expenditure	6,951		
	12,426		12,426

WORKINGS

(1)   Bar Trading account

Sales		10,243
Opening stock	943	
Purchases	7,306	
	8,249	
less Closing stock	1,100	7,149
Gross profit		3,094

(2)   Subscriptions account

1984			1984		
Jan. 1	Balance b/d	92	Jan. 1	Balance b/d	106
Dec. 31	Income and Expenditure	760	Dec. 31	Receipts	809
Dec. 31	Balance c/d	86	Dec. 31	Balance c/d	23
		938			938
1985			1985		
Jan. 1	Balance b/d	23	Jan. 1	Balance b/d	86

(b) Subscriptions in arrears is an item of income due *to* us at the balance sheet date and is therefore treated as a *debtor*. Light and heat owing is an item of expenditure due *by* us at the balance sheet date and is therefore treated as a *creditor*. Subscriptions in advance, conversely, is an amount prepaid *to* us and is therefore a *creditor*. Insurance prepaid is an amount prepaid *by* us and is therefore a *debtor*.

Question 15.3

The treasurer of the Downtown Club keeps its accounts on the double-entry system.
The following were the balances in the books at 31 March 1983, omitting only the General Fund Account (the Club's 'Capital Account').

	£
Overdrawn balance at the bank	622
Miscellaneous expenses	1,885
Members' subscriptions	1,625
Loans to members	520
Expenses of dances and socials	2,424
Equipment (cost)	3,650
Owing to suppliers of refreshments	392
Provision for depreciation of equipment	1,430

Sale of tickets for dances and socials	2,260
Cash in hand	320
Donations received	120

You are asked to prepare the trial balance at 31 March 1983, the General Fund Account being included as the balance figure. (OLE)

Answer 15.3

	£	£
Overdrawn balance at bank		622
Miscellaneous expenses	1,885	
Members' subscriptions		1,625
Loans to members	520	
Expenses of dances and socials	2,424	
Equipment (cost)	3,650	
Owing to suppliers of refreshments		392
Provision for depreciation of equipment		1,430
Sale of tickets for dances and socials		2,260
Cash in hand	320	
Donations received		120
General Fund account		2,350
	£8,799	£8,799

16 Partnership Accounts: 1

16.1 Definition

A partnership is a relationship between persons carrying on business in common with a view of profit. A key feature is. that each partner accepts full liability for the debts of the partnership, which means that if the business becomes insolvent, the partners are liable for the full debts of the business in the same way as a sole trader. However, if one partner is unable to meet his share of the debts, it must be met by the other partners.

16.2 The partnership agreement

It is advisable for the partners to draw up an agreement covering the following areas:

(i) *Capital*. How much each should contribute and leave in the business.
(ii) *Profit sharing*. One partner may be entitled to a greater share of the profits because he has more experience or is doing a greater share of the work.
(iii) *Salaries*. One or more partners may be entitled to a salary because of the work they are performing.
(iv) *Interest on capital*. This might be appropriate where one or more partners is contributing a materially greater sum than others.
(v) *Drawings*. The agreement should cover the amount of profits that may be withdrawn and may further discourage drawings by charging interest on them.

Any points not covered in the partnership agreement are decided by reference to the Partnership Act 1890, which states:

(i) Profits are shared equally.
(ii) No partnership salaries.
(iii) Partners shall receive no interest on capital but should receive 5 per cent interest per annum on any loans to the business.

In many ways the accounts of partnerships are similar to accounts for sole traders, but we shall now look at the areas in which they differ.

16.3 Capital accounts

In sole traders' accounts we have one capital account, whereas with partnership accounts we need a separate capital account for each partner. This will record the capital introduced by the partner and act as a permanent record of the capital contributed to the business by each partner.

16.4 Partners' current accounts

Partner's current accounts will record many of the transactions that are entered on the capital account in the sole trader's books. The current account will be credited with the partner's share of the profits of the business together with any interest and salary due to him. The current account will be debited with any drawings by the partners which will be transferred from the drawings account at the end of each accounting period.

16.5 Partners' loan accounts

If the business is short of cash, a partner may make a temporary loan to the partnership. This will be recorded in a separate loan account, although any interest to which the partner is entitled will normally be credited to his current account.

16.6 Profit and loss appropriation account

In a sole trader's books the profit and loss account balance representing the net profit of the business is transferred to the owner's capital account. In a partnership, as we have seen, the division of the profit will include accounting for salaries, interest on capital and the agreed profit-sharing ratio. To deal with these items, we extend the profit and loss account to create a further section or account, namely the appropriation account.

The net profit from the profit and loss account is carried down to the credit of the appropriation account. The next step is to debit the appropriation account and credit the individual partners' current accounts with any salary and interest to which they are entitled. If any interest is chargeable on drawings, this will be debited to the partners' current accounts and credited to the appropriation account. Finally, the remaining balance on the appropriation account will be distributed to the partners in the agreed profit-sharing ratio by debiting the appropriation account and crediting the partners' current accounts.

You should realise that interest on loans is an expense of the partnership, not an appropriation of profit, and therefore belongs in the profit and loss account proper and not in the appropriation account.

16.7 Worked examples

Example 16.1

(a) What is the purpose of the appropriation account when compiling the final accounts of a partnership?
(b) Black, White and Grey are in partnership and share profits and losses in the ratio of 3:2:1, respectively. From the following information prepare:

(i) the appropriation account for the partnership,
(ii) the partners' current accounts as they appear in the ledger.

		£
Net profit for year		24,000
Capital		
Black	12,000	
White	6,000	
Grey	10,000	28,000
Loan account		
Grey		10,000
Current accounts		
Black		4,000 (DR)
White		3,000 (CR)
Grey		5,000 (CR)
Partnership salaries		
Black	8,000	
White	10,000	18,000
Drawings		
Black	5,000	
White	10,000	15,000
Interest on drawings		
Black	600	
White	900	1,500

Interest on partners' capital is allowed at 10 per cent per annum. Interest on Grey's loan is at 20 per cent per annum.

Solution 16.1

(a) Refer to text. To show the allocation of the profit to the partners in accordance with the partnership agreement.

(b) (i)

Profit and loss appropriation account of Black, White and Grey for the year ended . . .

		£
Net profit (less loan interest deducted in profit		
and loss account) (£24,000 − £2,000)		22,000
Interest on drawings		1,500
		23,500
Interest on capital		
Black (10 per cent × £12,000)	1,200	
White (10 per cent × £6,000)	600	
Grey (10 per cent × £10,000)	1,000	2,800
		20,700
Salaries		
Black	8,000	
White	10,000	18,000
		2,700
Residual profits		
Black ($\frac{1}{2}$ × £2,700)	1,350	
White ($\frac{1}{3}$ × £2,700)	900	
Grey ($\frac{1}{6}$ × £2,700)	450	£ 2,700

(ii)

Partners' current accounts

	Black £	White £	Grey £		Black £	White £	Grey £
Balance b/d	4,000			Balance b/d		3,000	5,000
Interest on drawings	600	900		Interest on loan			2,000
Drawings	5,000	10,000		Interest on capital	1,200	600	1,000
Balance c/d	950	3,600	8,450	Salaries	8,000	10,000	
				Residual profits	1,350	900	450
	10,550	14,500	8,450		10,550	14,500	8,450
				Balance b/d	950	3,600	8,450

Example 16.2

Wood and Garner are in partnership as accountants, with capitals of £25,000 for Wood and £15,000 for Garner.

The partners have agreed to allow interest on capital at 9 per cent per annum and share profits/losses three-fifths Wood and two-fifths Garner.

The firm's accounts show the following balances at 31 August 1982, after preparation of the profit and loss account for the year ended on that date.

	£
Cash and bank	8,565
Fees receivable	6,800
Staff salaries owing	2,460
Premises	33,375
Office equipment at cost	5,000
Provision for depreciation of equipment	3,000
Net trading profit for the year (before partners' items)	15,700
Drawings for the year — Wood	6,000
— Garner	3,200
Current accounts at 1 September 1981 — Wood (debit)	520
— Garner (credit)	2,300

Additional information.

Garner used his home for business purposes and it has been agreed that £700 per annum running expenses be allowed. No entries have been made in the books.

REQUIRED

(a) (i) The profit and loss appropriation account and the partners' current accounts for the year ended 31 August 1982.   [7 marks]

(ii) A balance sheet as at 31 August 1982.   [7 marks]

(b) Comments on why partners might agree to:
   (i) allow interest on capital;
   (ii) charge interest on drawings.   [4 marks]

132

Solution 16.2

(a) (i)

Profit and loss appropriation account of Wood and Garner for year ended 31 August 1982

		£
Net profit (less £700 allowance to Garner charged in profit and loss account)		15,000
Interest on capital		
Wood (9% × £25,000)	2,250	
Garner (9% × £15,000)	1,350	3,600
		11,400
Residual profits		
Wood ($\frac{3}{5}$ × £11,400)	6,840	
Garner ($\frac{2}{5}$ × £11,400)	4,560	11,400

Partners' current accounts

	Wood £	Garner £		Wood £	Garner £
Balance b/d	520		Balance b/d		2,300
Drawings	6,000	3,200	Allowance		700
			Interest on capital	2,250	1,350
Balance c/d	2,570	5,710	Residual profits	6,840	4,560
	9,090	8,910		9,090	8,910
			Balance c/d	2,570	5,710

(ii)

Balance sheet of Wood and Garner as at 31 August 1982

Fixed Assets		£	
Premises		33,375	
Office equipment		2,000	
		35,375	
Current Assets			
Fees receivable	6,800		
Cash and bank	8,565		
	15,365		
less Current Liabilities			
Salaries owing	2,460		
Working capital		12,905	
Net Assets		£48,280	
Capital Accounts			
Wood		25,000	
Garner		15,000	
		40,000	
Current Accounts			
Wood	2,570		
Garner	5,710	8,280	
		£48,280	

(b) (i) Refer to Section 16.2. Reward partner contributing more capital than other partners.

(ii) Refer to Section 16.2. Discourage withdrawals.

Example 16.3

T. Edwards and R. Jones decided to start a retail grocery business. They started to make their arrangements on 1 March 1984, intending to open their store seven days later.

During the first week the following arrangements were made:

A bank account was opened into which each partner paid his agreed capital.

		£
	T. Edwards	120,000
	R. Jones	150,000
1984		
1 March	The purchase of premises was completed and a cheque drawn in full settlement	251,400
	The cheque for the purchase of the premises included an amount to cover rates paid in advance by the vendor	1,400
	T. Edwards made over to the business a delivery van which he owned	7,000
	Furniture from a business previously owned by R. Jones was delivered as part of Jones' capital	10,000
2 March	Stock was purchased and paid for immediately by cheque	10,000
	Additional furniture and fittings purchased and paid for by cheque	5,600
3 March	T. Edwards suddenly changed his mind and with the agreement of R. Jones withdrew all his capital by cheque	127,000
	S. Williams agreed to take T. Edward's place and paid into the business bank account as his capital	150,000
	S. Williams brought into the business a second delivery van valued at	9,000
	Tax and insurance on vans paid to 28 February 1985 by cheque	1,000
	Annual insurance premium on premises paid by cheque	3,000
4 March	Additional stock bought on credit	7,500

(a) Write up the bank account for the first four days.

(b) Write up the capital accounts of T. Edwards, R. Jones and S. Williams.

(c) Prepare the opening Balance Sheet of the business as on 8 March 1984.

(L)

Solution 16.3

(a)

Bank

		£			£
Mar. 1	Capital Edwards	120,000	Mar. 1	Premises	250,000
Mar. 1	Capital Jones	150,000	Mar. 1	Rates	1,400
Mar. 3	Capital Williams	150,000	Mar. 2	Purchases	10,000
			Mar. 2	Furniture and fittings	5,600
			Mar. 3	Capital Jones	127,000
			Mar. 3	Vehicle expenses	1,000
			Mar. 3	Insurance	3,000
			Mar. 8	Balance c/d	22,000
		420,000			420,000
Mar. 8	Balance b/d	22,000			

(b)

Capital

		Edwards £	Jones £	Williams £			Edwards £	Jones £	Williams £
Mar. 1	Bank	127,000			Mar. 1	Bank	120,000	150,000	
					Mar. 1	Delivery van	7,000		
					Mar. 1	Furniture		10,000	
					Mar. 3	Bank			150,000
Mar. 8	Balance c/d		160,000	159,000	Mar. 3	Delivery van			9,000
		127,000	160,000	159,000			127,000	160,000	159,000
					Mar. 8	Balance b/d		160,000	159,000

(c)
Balance sheet of Jones and Williams at 8 March 1984

	£	£
Fixed Assets		
Premises		250,000
Furniture		15,600
Delivery vans		16,000
		281,600
Current Assets		
Stock	17,500	
Prepayments (1)	5,400	
Bank	22,000	
	44,900	
less Current Liabilities		
Creditors	7,500	37,400
		£319,000
Capital Accounts		
Jones		160,000
Williams		159,000
		£319,000

NOTE

(1) Prepayments reflects payments for rates £1,400, van tax and insurance £1,000 and premises insurance £3,000. The few days which have expired on these items and should therefore be expensed in the profit and loss account have been ignored.

16.8 Further exercises

Question 16.1

Edgar and Edward are partners in a small private hotel. After preparing a trading and profit and loss account for the year ended 31 December 1984, the following balances remain in their books:

		£	£
Capital	Edgar		30,000
	Edward		30,000
Current accounts	Edgar		750
	Edward	250	
Fixed assets	Total	70,000	
Net current assets		7,500	
Net profit for year			23,000
Drawings in cash:	Edgar	2,400	
	Edward	3,600	
		83,750	83,750

When preparing the profit and loss account, no account had been taken of the following:

(i) Private accommodation occupied by the partners in the hotel valued at £3,000 each per annum.

(ii) Repairs paid for Edgar's private car £750 from the firm's bank account and included in the business expenses.

(iii) Mrs Edgar and Mrs Edward work in the hotel and are entitled to salaries:

Mrs Edgar   £3,000

Mrs Edward   £4,000

These salaries have not been paid.

(iv) The partners agree that £5,000 each of the profits should be transferred to their capital accounts so that the total of the capital should equal the value of the fixed assets.

Profits and losses are to be shared equally.

Prepare

(a) an account showing the correct net profit

(b) an appropriation account

(c) the partners' current accounts.

(L)

Answer 16.1

(a)

	£
Net profit as given	23,000
add (i) reimbursement for private accommodation	6,000
(ii) repairs to private motor car	750
	29,750
less (iii) salaries due	7,000
Adjusted net profit	£22,750

(b)

Profit and loss appropriation account of Edgar and Edward for year ended 31 December 1984

		£
		£
Net profit		22,750
Transfers to capital accounts		
Edgar	5,000	
Edward	5,000	10,000
		12,750
Residual profits		
Edgar	6,375	
Edward	6,375	£12,750

(c)

Partners' current accounts

	Edgar £	Edward £		Edgar £	Edward £
Balance b/d		250	Balance b/d	750	
Drawings	2,400	3,600	Residual profits	6,375	6,375
Private accommodation	3,000	3,000			
Private car repairs	750				
Balance c/d	975		Balance c/d		475
	7,125	6,850		7,125	6,850
Balance b/d		475	Balance b/d	975	

Question 16.2

Messrs Fairway and Rough, partners in a consultancy business, have the following balances in their books at 31 December 1984 (after extraction of the trading and profit and loss accounts):

	£
capital accounts (1 January 1984)	
Fairway	20,000
Rough	25,000
current accounts (1 January 1984)	
Fairway	4,200 Cr
Rough	2,060 Dr
drawings (for the year ended 31 December 1984)	
Fairway	12,000
Rough	15,000
motor van at cost	6,000
provision for depreciation on motor van	4,500
premises	50,000
cash at bank	3,298
wages accrued	1,968
debtors	3,210
bank loan (repayable in 1986)	15,000
interest on bank loan owing	600
net trading profit	20,300
interest on drawings	
Fairway	200
Rough	900

The partners had agreed to allow 8% interest on capital and to share remaining profits equally.

REQUIRED
    (a) For the year ended 31 December 1984:
        (i) the profit and loss appropriation account of the partnership;   [3 marks]
        (ii) each partner's current account.   [6 marks]
    (b) The balance sheet of the partnership as at 31 December 1984.   [8 marks]
                                           (AEB)

Answer 16.2

(a)

(i) Messrs Fairway and Rough Profit and Loss appropriation account for year ended 31 December 1984

		£	
Net trading profit			20,300
add Interest on drawings	Fairway	200	
	Rough	900	1,100
			21,400
less Interest on capital	Fairway	1,600	
	Rough	2,000	3,600
			17,800
Residual profits	Fairway	8,900	
	Rough	8,900	£17,800

(ii) Partners' current accounts

	Fairway £	Rough £		Fairway £	Rough £
Dec. 31 Balance b/d		2,060	Dec. 31 Balance b/d	4,200	
Dec. 31 P. L. appropr'n			Dec. 31 P. L. appropr'n		
(interest on drawings)	200	900	(interest)	1,600	2,000
Drawings	12,000	15,000	Dec. 31 P. L. appropr'n		
			(residual profit)	8,900	8,900
Dec. 31 Balance c/d	2,500		Dec. 31 Balance c/d		7,060
	14,700	17,960		14,700	17,960
1985			1985		
Jan. 1 Balance b/d		7,060	Jan. 1 Balance b/d	2,500	

(b)

Messrs Fairway and Rough balance sheet at 31 December 1986

		£	
Fixed Assets			
Premises		50,000	
Motor van (£6,000 – £4,500)		1,500	
		51,500	
Current Assets			
Debtors	3,210		
Cash at bank	3,298		
	6,508		
less Current Liabilities			
Creditors (£1,968 + £600)	2,568		
Working Capital		3,940	
Net Assets		£55,440	
Financed by			
Capital Fairway		20,000	
Rough		25,000	
		45,000	
Current accounts Fairway	2,500		
Rough	(7,060)	(4,560)	
Bank loan		15,000	
		£55,440	

Question 16.3

Spiros and Zorba are equal partners in a Greek takeaway food business. The business commenced on 1 January 1983, when each partner contributed £10,000 capital. For the first year it was agreed that partners be allowed 10 per cent interest on capital, a salary of £8,000 each, the remaining profits being shared equally.

The balances in the firm's books at 31 December 1983, with the exception of the partners' current accounts, were:

premises £15,500; fittings and equipment £6,800; creditors £2,432; stock £520; balance at bank £6,390; cash in hand £86; capital – Spiros £10,000; capital – Zorba £10,000.

During the year each partner withdrew his salary from the business.

REQUIRED

(a) Preparation of
(i) a closing statement of affairs in simple form, to ascertain the balance of each partner's current account at 31 December 1983;
(ii) the current account of Spiros for year ended 31 December 1983;
(iii) the balance sheet of the partnership as at 31 December 1983, distinguishing between fixed and current assets and current liabilities and showing working capital *within* the balance sheet. [*16 marks*]
(b) (i) One reason why partners might agree to charge interest on drawings.
(ii) An explanation of how interest on drawings of £400 each would be treated in the final accounts of Spiros and Zorba. [*4 marks*]

Answer 16.3

(a) (i)
Statement of affairs of Spiros and Zorba at 31 December 1983

	£
Premises	15,500
Fittings and equipment	6,800
Stock	520
Bank	6,390
Cash	86
	29,296
less Creditors	2,432
Net Assets	£26,864
Capital account balances	20,000
Current account balances (balancing figures) (1)	
Spiros 3,432	
Zorba 3,432	6,864
	£26,864

NOTE

(1) Since both partners are entitled to the same interest and residual profit and both have the same drawings, their current accounts must be equal.

(ii)

Spiros current account

	£		£
Drawings	8,000	Salary	8,000
Balance c/d (as (i))	3,432	Interest	1,000
		Residual profit (balancing figure)	2,432
	11,432		11,432
		Balance b/d	3,432

(iii)
Balance sheet of Spiros and Zorba at 31 December 1983

Fixed Assets		£
Premises		15,500
Fittings and equipment		6,800
		22,300
Current Assets		
Stock	520	
Bank	6,390	
Cash in hand	86	
	6,996	
less Current Liabilities		
Creditors	2,432	
Working Capital		4,564
Net Assets		£26,864
Financed by		
Capital		
Spiros		10,000
Zorba		10,000
		20,000
Current accounts		
Spiros	3,432	
Zorba	3,432	6,864
		£26,864

(b)

(i) Refer to Section 16.2. Discourage withdrawals.

(ii) Refer to Section 16.6. Dr. current accounts, cr. profit and loss appropriation account.

Question 16.4

The information given below relates to the partnership of J. Hale and D. Harty

Capital, 1 April 1982: J. Hale	£18,000
D. Harty	£12,500
New capital introduced on 1 October 1982 by D. Harty	£2,500

Profit-sharing arrangements:
  Salary to D. Harty, £8,000 per annum;
  Interest on capital, 12 per cent per annum;
  Remaining profit to be shared equally.
Profit for the year to 31 March 1983, before deducting partners' interest
  and salary: £32,600.

You are asked to prepare the Appropriation Section of the partnership's Profit and Loss Account for the year ended 31 March 1983.

[12]

(OLE)

Answer 16.4

Profit and loss appropriation account of Hale and Harty for year ended 31 December 1983

		£
Net profit		32,600
Salary Harty		8,000
		24,600
Interest on capital		
Hale (12 per cent × £18,000)	2,160	
Harty (12 per cent × £12,500 plus $\frac{6}{12}$ × 12 per cent × £2,500)	1,650	3,810
		20,790
Residual profit		
Hale ($\frac{1}{2}$ × £20,790)	10,395	
Harty ($\frac{1}{2}$ × £20,790)	10,395	£20,790

Question 16.5

(a) (i) What is the purpose of the appropriation section of the profit and loss account to a partnership? [*1 mark*]
   (ii) Name four items that can be found in the appropriation section and explain, in each case, where the double entry would be found. [*8 marks*]
(b) A partner withdraws goods valued at £200 cost price.
   (i) How would this item be entered in the ledger accounts? [*2 marks*]
   (ii) How would these drawings be shown in the final accounts? [*1 mark*]
(c) In the absence of a partnership agreement, how would partners resolve disputes with respect to:
   (i) share of profit;
   (ii) partners' salaries;
   (iii) interest on loan by a partner? [*3 marks*]

Answer 16.5

(a) (i) Refer to Section 16.6 to show appropriation of profit to partners.
   (ii) Refer to Section 16.6.
      Salaries: dr. appropriation account, cr. current account;
      interest on drawings: dr. current account, cr. appropriation account;
      interest on capital: dr. appropriation account, cr. current account;
      residual profit: dr. appropriation account, cr. current account.
(b) (i) dr. drawing's account, cr. purchases.
   (ii) Deduction from purchases and debit to current account.
(c) All as Partnership Act 1980:
   (i) equally;
   (ii) none;
   (iii) 5 per cent per annum.

17 Partnership Accounts: 2

17.1 Introduction

In Chapter 16 we looked at examples where the partnership had commenced as a new business. We shall now examine the situation where a partnership is formed by the amalgamation of two existing businesses. In a simple case where the partners bring in cash or assets the entries are the same as those illustrated in worked example 16.3 in Chapter 16 — that is,

Dr. Asset account
   Cr. Partner's capital account

The asset account being debited would be cash, fixtures or delivery van, for example, according to the asset introduced. The disadvantage which could arise for a new partner would be in the case where the business is worth more than the total of the individual assets which the partner has introduced into the business. For example, a partner may introduce assets as follows:

	£
Premises	50,000
Fixtures	8,000
Stock	10,000
	£68,000

The business may, however, for reasons examined below, be worth £100,000. The difference between the worth of the business and the value of its total assets, in this case £32,000 (£100,000 less £68,000), we call goodwill.

17.2 Goodwill

Having defined goodwill above, we shall now look at some of the reasons why goodwill exists and, more important, why it has some value. Remember we are basically looking for reasons why a business is worth more than the value of its individual assets. Another way of stating the problem is: why would a person pay more for a business than it would cost to buy individual assets similar to those owned by the business?

(i) The existing trade built up by the business, especially if the business has a good reputation. This reputation will often mean that the sales and profits will continue for some time after the business has been taken over. When a new business is started, the trade has to be built up over a period of time and often will not make profits from day 1.

(ii) The labour force and management of a business is an asset which does not show in the balance sheet. This may be particularly valuable where skills are rare or morale is high. When a new business commences, labour has to be trained and staff relationships built up.

(iii) The business may be in a particular location which has advantages, and new premises, for example, could not be found in that area.

We must appreciate that goodwill can exist in a business of any size. In the large businesses it will often be due to the reputation of the company, whereas with a sole trader it will depend more on the reputation of its owner.

There are practical problems with regard to the valuation of goodwill which result in long negotiations. There are several methods for calculating the value of goodwill. However, examination questions at this level will only involve the accounting treatment rather than its valuation.

17.3   Goodwill on amalgamation of businesses

The accounting treatment of goodwill on amalgamation of businesses involves opening a goodwill account. We then treat goodwill in the same way as we record any other asset brought into the business by a partner — that is,

Dr. Goodwill account
    Cr. Partner's capital account

The balance on the goodwill account will remain on the books as an asset of the business and appear as an asset on its balance sheet. This will apply until the partners decide to write off the asset, which we consider below in Section 17.5.

17.4   Goodwill on admission of new partner

We have seen how a business once it has been trading for some time builds up an asset goodwill. This will not normally be recorded in the books, since there would be little point, it is difficult to value and it is not a physical asset. However, we saw in Section 17.1 that the valuation of goodwill is important when two existing businesses amalgamate. Another case when its value is important is when a new partner is admitted to a business. The existing partners will have built up goodwill in the partnership but it will not appear as such on the balance sheet. If the new partner is admitted without due recognition of this, then the new partner immediately shares in all future profits and benefits from that goodwill built up by existing partners. It will therefore be usual to value goodwill on the admission of a new partner. The accounting entries to create goodwill are

Dr. Goodwill account
    Cr. Partners' capital accounts

Unless otherwise stated, the allocation of goodwill to the partners' capital accounts will be according to the profit-sharing ratio of the partnership before the admission of the new partner.

17.5   Writing off goodwill

We have looked at how goodwill arises in the books of a business either on the taking over of an existing business or when it is created on the admission of a new partner. We stated in Section 17.2 that during the normal course of events a business will not show an asset goodwill on its books. In fact its very appearance on a balance sheet can be off-putting to creditors and prospective purchasers because of its lack of tangibility. For this reason the partners may decide either immediately or at some future date to write off that goodwill. As with its creation, unless otherwise stated, it will be written off according to profit-sharing ratios, but those of the new partnership rather than the old. The accounting entries to eliminate goodwill will be

Dr. Partners' capital accounts
Cr. Goodwill account

17.6 Worked examples

Example 17.1

C. Walters and R. Strange are the proprietors of two separate retail businesses. Their Balance Sheets on 31 December 1983 are given below.

C. Walter Balance Sheet as at 31 December 1983

	£		£
Capital	86,880	Premises	65,000
Creditors	2,140	Delivery vans	15,000
		Stock	7,400
		Bank	1,500
		Cash	120
	89,020		89,020

R. Strange Balance Sheet as at 31 December 1983

	£		£
Capital	98,410	Premises	80,000
Creditors	1,470	Furniture	12,000
		Stock	4,700
		Debtors	1,400
		Bank	1,700
		Cash	80
	99,880		99,880

They decide to amalgamate into a partnership running two branches from 1 January 1984. Profits and losses will be shared equally.
The following valuations and revaluations were agreed by the partners:

	C. Walters	R. Strange
	£	£
Goodwill	20,000	15,000
Premises	120,000	90,000
Furniture		8,000

R. Strange will not bring his debtors into the partnership.

(a) Calculate the capital each partner is introducing into the business.
(b) Write off the goodwill.
(c) Set out the Balance Sheet of the new business as at 1 January 1984, after writing off the goodwill.

(d) On 2 January 1984 Walters and Strange agreed to bring in extra or take out cash so that their capitals should be equal at £125,000. This was done immediately.

Write up the partners' capital accounts from 1 January 1984 showing the capital adjustments, and the bank columns of the cash books showing the resultant bank balance.

[24 marks]

(Assume no other transactions take place).

(L)

Solution 17.1

(a) Capital introduced

	C. Walters	R. Strange
	£	£
Premises	120,000	90,000
Furniture		8,000
Delivery vans	15,000	
Goodwill	20,000	15,000
Stock	7,400	4,700
Bank	1,500	1,700
Cash	120	80
	164,020	119,480
less creditors	2,140	1,470
	£161,880	£118,010

(b)

	Dr.	Cr.
C. Walters capital account	17,500	
R. Strange capital account	17,500	
Goodwill account		35,000

(c)
Balance sheet of Walters and Strange as at 1 January 1984

		£
Fixed Assets		
Premises		210,000
Furniture		8,000
Delivery vans		15,000
		233,000
Current Assets		
Stock	12,100	
Bank	3,200	
Cash	200	
	15,500	
less Current Liabilities		
Creditors	3,610	
Working Capital		11,890
Net Assets		£244,890
Financed by		
Capital account		
C. Walters		144,380
R. Strange		100,510
		£244,890

(d)

Capital accounts

1984		C. Walters £	R. Strange £	1984		C. Walters £	R. Strange £
Jan. 1	Goodwill	17,500	17,500	Jan. 2	Various assets	161,880	118,010
Jan. 2	Bank	19,380		Jan. 2	Bank		24,490
Jan. 2	Balance c/d	125,000	125,000				
		161,880	142,500			161,880	142,500
				Jan. 2	Balance b/d	125,000	125,000

Bank

1984		£	1984		£
Jan. 1	Capital C. Walters	1,500	Jan. 2	Capital C. Walters	19,380
Jan. 1	Capital R. Strange	1,700	Jan. 2	Balance c/d	8,310
Jan. 2	Capital R. Strange	24,490			
		27,690			27,690
Jan. 2	Balance b/d	8,310			

Example 17.2

(a) Define goodwill and explain how it would arise in a partnership.

(b) Newman and Redford are partners and share profits and losses equally. The balances remaining open in the books of their business as at 31 May were as follows:

	£
Newman's capital account	12,000
Redford's capital account	10,000
Stock	7,000
Debtors	8,000
Creditors	20,000
Premises	30,000
Machinery	15,000
Newman's current account	5,000 (CR)
Redford's current account	2,000 (CR)
Cash in hand	5,000
Bank overdraft	16,000

On 1 June 1983 the partners admitted Woodward as a partner on terms that she brought in capital of £12,000 (which was paid directly into the bank account) and a premium of £20,000 to be entered to a goodwill account and shared between the original partners' capital in the same proportion as they shared profits.

From the above information you are required to prepare the balance sheet for the new partnership as at 1 June 1983.

Solution 17.2

(a) Refer to Sections 17.1 and 17.2.

(b)

Balance sheet of Newman, Redford and Woodward as at 1 June 1983

Fixed Assets			£
Premises			30,000
Machinery			15,000
Goodwill			20,000
			65,000
Current Assets			
Stock		7,000	
Debtors		8,000	
Cash in hand		5,000	
		20,000	
less Current Liabilities			
Creditors	20,000		
Bank overdraft (£16,000 − £12,000)	4,000	24,000	
Working Capital			(4,000)
Net Assets			£61,000
Financed by			
Capital Accounts			
Newman			22,000
Redford			20,000
Woodward			12,000
			54,000
Current Accounts			
Newman		5,000	
Redford		2,000	7,000
			£61,000

17.7 Further exercises

Question 17.1

Balance Sheet as at 31 March 1983

	£		£
Capital A	25,000	Fixed assets	50,000
B	25,000	Current assets	3,120
Creditors	3,120		
	53,120		53,120

The above Balance Sheet is a summary of the state of affairs of A and B partners sharing profits and losses equally.

They decide to admit C as a partner with effect from 1 April 1983. C will bring in cash of £14,000 and the new business will share profits between A, B and C in the ratio of 2:2:1.

A, B and C agree the goodwill of the existing business of A and B to be £15,000.

(a) Draft the journal entries required to incorporate the goodwill in the account of A and B.

(b) Show, using journal entries, the introduction of C's cash.

(c) Draft the journal entries to write off the goodwill between the three partners of the new business.

(d) Set out the opening Balance Sheet of the new business on 1 April 1983, after goodwill has been written off.

(e) There were two applicants for admission to the business, C with £14,000 in cash, and D with fixed assets valued at £9,000 and a goodwill connection valued at £5,000.

Set out the Balance Sheet as it would have appeared on 1 April 1983 on the assumption that D would have been admitted on the same terms as C. (Goodwill is not to appear in the balance sheet.)

(f) On purely business considerations, why did A and B prefer C to D?

(L)

Answer 17.1

(a)

	Dr. £	Cr. £
A Capital account		7,500
B Capital account		7,500
Goodwill account	15,000	

(b)

Cash	14,000	
C Capital account		14,000

(c)

A Capital account	6,000	
B Capital account	6,000	
C Capital account	3,000	
Goodwill account		15,000

(d)

Balance sheet of A, B and C as at 1 April 1983

		£
Fixed Assets		50,000
Current Assets (£14,000 + £3,120)	17,120	
less Creditors	3,120	
Working Capital		14,000
Net Assets		£64,000
Financed by		
Capital A		26,500
Capital B		26,500
Capital C		11,000
		£64,000

(e)

Balance sheet of A, B and C as at 1 April 1983

		£
Fixed Assets		59,000
Current Assets	3,120	
less Creditors	3,120	
Working Capital		0
Net Assets		£59,000
Financed by		
Capital A		24,500
Capital B		24,500
Capital C		10,000
		£59,000

(f) (i) No cost of goodwill.
    (ii) Business in need of liquid funds.

Question 17.2

Martina and Beryl are partners sharing profits and losses in the ratio of 3 : 1.
On 31 May 1985 the following balances remained in their books after completion of the trading and profit and loss accounts for the year:

	£000		£000
Fixed assets	305	Capital Martina	200
Stock	10	Beryl	100
Debtors	7	Creditors	25
Bank	3		
	325		325

On that day they agreed to admit Catherine as a partner. The new partnership will share profits and losses as follows: Martina $\frac{1}{2}$, Beryl $\frac{1}{4}$, Catherine $\frac{1}{4}$.

Catherine brought into the business cash £100,000 and a goodwill connection valued at £12,000.

It was agreed that the goodwill of Martina and Beryl should be £60,000.

Goodwill will not remain in the books after the admission has been completed.

(a) Write up the capital accounts of the three partners and compile the trial balance of the new business after the goodwill has been written off.   [*11 marks*]
(b) Compare the working capital of the new business with that of Martina and Beryl and suggest reasons for their agreement to the admission of Catherine.   [*2 marks*]
    (L)

Answer 17.2

(a)
Capital accounts

		Martina	Beryl	Cath.			Martina	Beryl	Cath.
May 31	Goodwill (2)	36	18	18	May 31	Balance b/d	200	100	
May 31	Balance c/d	209	97	94	May 31	Goodwill (1)	45	15	12
						Cash			100
		245	115	112			245	115	112
					June 1	Balance b/d	209	97	94

WORKINGS
(1) Goodwill of Martina and Beryl credited to them in profit sharing ratio 3:1.
(2) Goodwill of existing partners   60
    Goodwill of Catherine   12

    To be written off in new profit sharing ratio   72

Trial balance (all figures £000s)

	£	£
Fixed Assets	305	
Stock	10	
Debtors	7	
Bank	103	
Capital Martina		209
Beryl		97
Catherine		94
Creditors		25
	425	425

(b)
Working capital (£000s)

	old	new
Stock	10	10
Debtors	7	7
Bank	3	103
	20	120
less Creditors	25	25
	£(5)	£95

Reasons for admission of new partner: (i) to increase liquidity as demonstrated above; (ii) to increase level of business, since Catherine has a valuable goodwill connection.

18 Manufacturing Accounts

18.1 Introduction

In the examples we have looked at so far, most businesses have been trading businesses. That is to say, they have purchased goods and resold them. We now look at what happens where instead of purchasing goods the business manufactures the goods itself. Simply stated, all of the costs incurred in connection with the cost of manufacturing are collected in the manufacturing account, which we prepare to ascertain the cost of finished production. Having ascertained the cost of finished production, we transfer this amount to the trading account, where it replaces the item 'purchases' which appears in the trading account of trading businesses.

We shall now examine the types of cost which appear in the manufacturing account.

18.2 Types of cost

(i) Direct materials are materials and components used to make up the products which the business is manufacturing.

(ii) Direct labour is the cost of labour that is directly involved in producing items of output.

(iii) Direct expenses are expenses which can be directly allocated to a particular unit of goods being made.

(iv) Factory overheads are other costs incurred in the factory which cannot be attributed to any specific output. Also referred to as indirect costs.

(v) Prime cost is the sum total of direct materials, direct labour and direct expenses.

(vi) Production cost is the prime cost plus overheads.

18.3 Opening and closing stocks

In previous examples we have seen how the opening and closing stocks were brought into the cost of sales calculation in the trading account. We shall now consider how this and other stocks affect the accounts of a manufacturing business. First of all, we must consider stocks of a manufacturing business in three categories: raw materials, work in progress and finished goods.

(a) Raw Materials

The raw materials used by a manufacturing business are part of the cost of production. In order to calculate the cost of materials used, we must consider our expenditure on raw material purchases and adjust that figure for opening and closing stocks. The calculation will be as follows:

	£
Opening stock of raw materials	x
add Purchases of raw materials	x
sub-total	S/T
less Closing stock of raw materials	(x)
Cost of raw materials consumed	T

(b) Work in Progress or Work in Process (WIP)

WIP represents partly manufactured goods, not yet completed, which are still being worked on at the accounting period end. There will be an element of raw material labour and possibly overhead included in its valuation. If we ignore the value of work in progress, our total cost of production will reflect, not the cost of finished production but the cost of finished and unfinished production. Since it is the cost of finished production which we wish to calculate, we must deduct the value of closing work in progress from our total cost of production. We carry forward the value of work in progress to the next accounting period and add it to that period's production costs. Our cost of finished production can therefore be calculated as follows:

		£
Total cost of production		x
Opening work in progress	x	
less Closing work in progress	(x)	x
Total cost of finished production		T

(c) Finished Goods

Finished goods is the value of goods completely manufactured and ready for resale, but which have not been sold at the end of the accounting period. These will be adjusted for in the trading account, just as we have in previous examples.

18.4 Transfer price of finished goods produced

In Section 18.1 we said that the cost of finished goods produced is transferred to the trading account, and this is the usual procedure. Some businesses, however, transfer to trading account a value which reflects the price which would have been paid to a supplier of those finished goods. The accounting treatment in this case is as follows:

Dr. Trading account
    Cr. Manufacturing account (with transfer value of finished goods)
Dr. Manufacturing account
    Cr. Profit and loss account (with balance remaining on the manufacturing account, which we term manufacturing profit)

This will result in the profit and loss account having transferred to it (a) manufacturing profit, (b) trading profit or gross profit.

18.5 Manufacturing accounts for separate products

If an examination question requires separate manufacturing accounts for different products, you should tackle it in the same way as a total manufacturing account and also follow the advice in Chapter 13 on departmental accounts.

18.6 Fixed and variable costs

A further classification of costs is as follows:

(i) Variable costs vary with the number of goods produced.
(ii) Fixed costs are the same total amount for a period of time regardless of the number of units produced.

Although, in general, variable costs are direct and fixed costs are indirect, we must not confuse the meaning of these classifications.

18.7 Worked examples

Example 18.1

G. Club is a manufacturer of spare parts and the following balances were some of those appearing in his books at 31 December 1984.

	£
Ordinary share capital	50,000
Stocks at 1 January 1984	
raw materials	11,000
work in progress	16,000
finished goods	20,090
Stocks at 31 December 1984	
raw materials	17,000
work in progress	18,000
finished goods	18,040
Wages	
direct manufacturing	203,080
factory supervisors'	13,325
general office	10,200
warehouse	19,300

Direct factory power	95,000
Heating and lighting	9,000
Purchase of raw materials	256,000
Carriage outwards	986
Plant and machinery	80,000
Premises	120,000
Returns inward	420
Office equipment	15,000
Rates	6,000
Administrative expenses	1,800
Debtors	14,000
Creditors	12,000
Cash in hand	3,662
Sales	800,290
Bank overdraft	25,641

REQUIRED

(a) For the year ended 31 December 1984, preparation of the manufacturing and trading account of G. Club, apportioning heating and lighting and rates: factory $\frac{1}{2}$, warehouse $\frac{1}{3}$ and office $\frac{1}{6}$. [*15 marks*]

Note: Not all of the balances listed at the beginning of the question will be needed in your solution, as you are NOT required to prepare a profit and loss account or a balance sheet.

(b) An explanation of the meaning of:
  (i) 'variable expense';
  (ii) 'fixed expense'.
  Illustrate your answer by providing **two** examples of each type of expense. [*5 marks*]
  (AEB)

Solution 18.1

(a)

Manufacturing account of G. Club for year ended 31 December 1984

		£
Raw materials		
Opening stock		11,000
Purchases		256,000
		267,000
less Closing stock		17,000
Cost of raw materials consumed		250,000
Manufacturing wages		203,080
Prime cost		453,080
Overheads		
Wages factory supervisors	13,325	
Power	95,000	
Heating and lighting ($\frac{1}{2}$)	4,500	
Rates ($\frac{1}{2}$)	3,000	115,825
		568,905
Work in progress adjustment		
Opening stock	16,000	
less Closing stock	18,000	(2,000)
Cost of finished goods produced		£566,905

154

Trading account of G. Club for year ended 31 December 1984

Sales		800,290
less Returns inward		420
		799,870
Opening stock of finished goods	20,090	
Cost of finished goods produced	566,905	
	586,995	
less Closing stock of finished goods	18,040	
	568,955	
Warehouse wages	19,300	
Heating and lighting ($\frac{1}{3}$)	3,000	
Rates ($\frac{1}{3}$)	2,000	
Cost of Sales		593,255
Gross profit		£206,615

(b) Refer to Section 18.6.
    (i) For example, factory power, raw materials.
    (ii) For example, factory rent, machinery depreciation.

Example 18.2

T. Morgan is the proprietor of a manufacturing business, making two products (Brand X and Brand Y). On 30 April 1982, the following Trial Balance was prepared:

	£	£
Trade debtors and trade creditors	32,950	11,680
Bank interest	4,300	
Cash discounts allowed	1,260	
Carriage outwards	12,750	
Manufacturing wages: Brand X	78,640	
Brand Y	66,900	
Sundry manufacturing expenses: Brand X	9,100	
Brand Y	10,250	
Office salaries	14,570	
Sundry office expenses	7,260	
Selling expenses	21,540	
Raw material purchases	88,500	
Sales: Brand X		189,940
Brand Y		165,870
Stocks, 1 May 1981: Raw materials	14,260	
Brand X	25,200	
Brand Y	17,900	
Land and buildings	61,000	
Machinery and plant	28,800	
Office equipment	4,640	
Vehicles	8,600	
Capital		118,870
Drawings	23,500	
Petty cash	340	
Bank overdraft		45,900
	532,260	532,260

You are asked to prepare T. Morgan's Manufacturing, Trading and Profit and Loss Account for the year to 30 April 1982, showing the net profit or loss made on each brand, and the Balance at 30 April 1982, taking the following into account:

(a) Stocks at 30 April 1982: Raw materials £22,400
                              Brand X   £21,300
                              Brand Y   £17,400

(b) Of the total cost of raw materials consumed in manufacturing, £46,300 applies to Brand X, and the remainder to Brand Y.

(c) Allow for depreciation at the following rates (all on book value): Machinery and plant 20 per cent, Vehicles 30 per cent, Office equipment 10 per cent. All the amounts are to be charged in equal proportions to Brand X and Brand Y. The vehicles are used for transporting goods to customers.

(d) Each brand is to be charged with one-half of any non-manufacturing expenses. [24]

(OLE)

Solution 18.2

Manufacturing account of T. Morgan for year ended 30 April 1982

	X £	Y £	Total £
Raw materials			
Opening stocks (1 May 1981)		14,260	
Purchases		88,500	
		102,760	
less Closing stocks (30 April 1981)		22,400	
Cost of raw materials used	46,300	34,060	80,360
Manufacturing wages	78,640	66,900	145,540
Sundry manufacturing expenses	9,100	10,250	19,350
Prime cost	134,040	111,210	245,250
Overheads			
Depreciation machinery and plant	2,880	2,880	5,760
Cost of production of finished goods	£136,920	114,090	251,010

Trading and profit and loss account of T. Morgan for year ended 30 April 1982

		X £		Y £		Total £
Sales		189,940		165,870		355,810
Opening stock (1 May 1981)	25,200		17,900		43,100	
Cost of production of finished goods	136,920		114,090		251,010	
	162,120		131,990		294,110	
less Closing stock (30 April 1982)	21,300		17,400		38,700	
Cost of sales		140,820		114,590		255,410
Gross profit		49,120		51,280		100,400
less						
Bank interest	2,150		2,150		4,300	
Cash discounts	630		630		1,260	
Office salaries	7,285		7,285		14,570	
Sundry office expenses	3,630		3,630		7,260	
Carriage outwards	6,375		6,375		12,750	
Selling expenses	10,770		10,770		21,540	
Depreciation vehicles	1,290		1,290		2,580	
Depreciation office equipment	232	32,362	232	32,362	464	64,724
Net profit		£16,758		£18,918		£35,676

Balance sheet of T. Morgan as at 30 April 1982

			£
Fixed Assets			
Land and buildings			61,000
Machinery and plant (£28,800 − £5,760)			23,040
Office equipment (£4,640 − £464)			4,176
Vehicles (£8,600 − £2,580)			6,020
			94,236
Current Assets			
Stock − raw materials	22,400		
− finished goods	38,700	61,100	
Debtors		32,950	
Petty cash		340	
		94,390	
less Current Liabilities			
Creditors	11,680		
Bank overdraft	45,900	57,580	
Working Capital			36,810
Net Assets			£131,046
Financed by			
Capital (balance 1 May 1981)			118,870
add net profit			35,676
			154,546
less drawings			23,500
Capital (balance 30 April 1982)			£131,046

18.8 Further exercises

Question 18.1

(a) J. Cook is the owner of a manufacturing business and on 31 December 1983 he supplies you with the following information extracted from his books:

RAW MATERIALS	£000
Purchases	600
Carriage on purchases	20
Stock 1 January 1983	65
Stock 31 December 1983	60

FINISHED GOODS	
Sales	1,200
Stock at Factory Cost 1 January 1983	120
Stock at Factory Cost 31 December 1983	110

WORK IN PROGRESS	
Stock at Factory Cost 1 January 1983	85
Stock at Factory Cost 31 December 1983	80

Factory Insurance Premiums paid for period from 1 January 1983 to 30 September 1983	6
Rent and Rates	10
Lighting and Heating	60

General Factory Expenses	4
Manufacturing Wages	350
Selling and Delivery Expenses	10

SALARIES

Office Management	18
Factory Management	12

Debtors	216
Creditors	120
Office Fixtures and Fittings at Cost	20
Factory Machinery at Cost	100
Premises at Cost	200
Cash in Hand and at Bank	30

NOTES

(1) Lighting and Heating AND Rent and Rates are to be apportioned between the Factory and Office Administration in the ratio of 3:2.
(2) Depreciation: Machinery at 10 per cent of cost.
   Office Fixtures and Fittings at 20 per cent of cost.
(3) Factory Insurance Premiums are due but unpaid at the same rate for 3 months ending 31 December 1983.

USING THE NECESSARY INFORMATION from the opposite page [i.e. above], PREPARE A MANUFACTURING ACCOUNT AND A TRADING ACCOUNT for the year 1983. The accounts must show CLEARLY LABELLED:
   (i) Cost of Raw Materials Consumed.
  (ii) Prime Cost.
 (iii) Cost of Goods Manufactured.
  (iv) Gross Profit.

DO NOT PREPARE A PROFIT AND LOSS ACCOUNT OR BALANCE SHEET
HEAD UP YOUR MONEY COLUMNS AS £000
DO NOT ADD "000" TO EVERY FIGURE   [*21*]

(b) CALCULATE the Manufacturing cost per unit if 40,000 units were manufactured during 1983.   [*1*]
(c) EXPLAIN the differences between:
   (i) DIRECT COSTS and INDIRECT COSTS
  (ii) FIXED COSTS and VARIABLE COSTS   [*4*]
                                                                  (SEB)

Answer 18.1

(a)
Manufacturing account of J. Cook for year ended 31 December 1983

			£000
Raw materials			
Opening stock (1 January 1983)		65	
Purchases	600		
add carriage on purchases	20	620	
		685	
less Closing stocks (31 December 1983)		60	
Cost of raw materials consumed			625
Manufacturing wages			350
Prime cost			975

Overheads

Factory insurance premiums (£6,000 + £2,000)	8	
Factory rent and rates	6	
Factory lighting and heating	36	
Factory general expenses	4	
Factory management salaries	12	
Depreciation of machinery	10	76
		1,051

Work in progress

Opening stock (1 January 1983)	85	
less Closing stock (31 December 1983)	80	
Increase in WIP		5
Cost of goods manufactured		£1,056

Trading account of J. Cook for year ended 31 December 1983

		£
Sales		1,200
Opening stock (1 January 1983)	120	
Cost of goods manufactured	1,056	
	1,176	
less Closing stock (31 December 1983)	110	
Cost of sales		1,066
Gross profit		£134

(b) $\dfrac{£1,056,000}{40,000} = £26.40$ per unit

(c) (i) Refer to Section 18.2.

(ii) Refer to Section 18.6.

Question 18.2

Mr R. Reed owns a small workshop in which he manufactures cricket bats in two qualities, 5 star and 3 star. The following information is provided from his records for the year to 31 March 1982.

Stocks at 1 April 1981:	£
Raw materials	3,860
Finished goods 5 star	1,225
3 star	3,200
Purchases of raw materials	124,514
Carriage on raw materials	320
Workshop wages 5 star	16,000
3 star	48,000
Workshop light and heat	1,300
Workshop general expenses	800
Workshop rent and rates	1,800
Raw materials returned to suppliers	480
Sales 5 star	100,000
3 star	200,000
Stocks at 31 March 1982:	
Raw materials	1,320
Finished goods 5 star	594
3 star	2,125

Workshop records show that, of the raw materials consumed in production in the year ended 31 March 1982, £50,894 was used in the production of 5 star and the remainder in the production of 3 star. All workshop costs not allocated are to be apportioned one-quarter to the production of 5 star and three-quarters to the production of 3 star.

REQUIRED

For the year ended 31 March 1982:

(a) a manufacturing account showing clearly the prime cost and the factory cost of goods manufactured for each grade of the product; [*10 marks*]

(b) a trading account for each grade of the product; [*5 marks*]

(c) a brief explanation of the significance of the factory cost of goods manufactured. [*2 marks*]

Note: You are recommended to adopt the columnar form of presentation for the manufacturing and trading accounts.

(AEB)

Answer 18.2

(a)
Manufacturing account of R. Read for the year ended 31 March 1982

	5 star		3 star		Total
	£		£		£
Raw materials					
Opening stock (1 April 1981)					3,860
Purchases				124,514	
add carriage				320	
				124,834	
less returns				480	124,354
					128,214
less Closing stock (31 March 1982)					1,320
Cost of raw material consumed		50,894		76,000	126,894
Workshop wages		16,000		48,000	64,000
Prime cost		66,894		124,000	190,894
Overheads					
Workshop light and heat	325		975		1,300
Workshop general expenses	200		600		800
Workshop rent and rates	450	975	1,350	2,925	1,800	3,900
Cost of finished production		£67,869		£126,925	£194,794

(b)
Trading account of R. Reed for the year ended 31 March 1982

	5 star		3 star		Total
	£		£		£
Sales		100,000		200,000	300,000
Opening stock (1 April 1981)	1,225		3,200		4,425
Cost of finished production	67,869		126,925		194,794
	69,094		130,125		199,219
less Closing stock (31 March 1982)	594		2,125		2,719
Cost of goods sold		68,500		128,000	196,500
Gross profit		£31,500		£72,000	£103,500

(c) Refer to Section 18.1.

Question 18.3

W. Wilkins manufactures concrete ornamental birdbaths in one standard pattern.
The following information relates to the manufacture of 1,000 birdbaths during the month ended 31 May 1984, and to his sales, during that month.

			£
1 May	Stock of finished birdbaths: 150 valued at		375
	Stock of: sand		100
		cement	1,300
		gravel chippings	70
	Purchases during month: sand		75
		cement	1,200
		gravel chippings	100
31 May	Stock of: sand		90
		cement	1,450
		gravel chippings	95
	Carriage inwards paid during month		85
	Workshop wages paid		900
	Workshop rent and rates		150
	Workshop heating and lighting		75
	Power used by mixing machines, etc.		140
	Water charges for mixer		25

During the month 1,000 birdbaths were completed and 950 sold for £3 each.

(a) Prepare a manufacturing account and a trading account for the month of May 1984. (Show clearly your calculations of the number and value of birdbaths in stock at the end of the month.)
(b) After having completed the accounts for the month W. Wilkins learns that his employees' union has negotiated a wage increase backdated to 1 May 1984. This will increase his wages bill for the month to £1,000. Re-calculate:

  (i) Prime cost,
  (ii) Cost of production,
  (iii) Value of closing stock,
  (iv) Cost of goods sold,
  (v) Gross profit.   (L)

Answer 18.3

(a)
Manufacturing account of W. Wilkins for the month ended 31 May 1984

		£
Raw materials		
Opening stock (1 May 1984)		1,470
Purchases	1,375	
add carriage inwards	85	1,460
		2,930
less Closing stock (31 May 1984)		1,635

Cost of raw materials consumed		1,295
Wages		900
Prime cost		2,195
Overheads		
Rent and rates	150	
Heating and lighting	75	
Power used	140	
Water charges	25	390
Cost of finished production		£2,585

Trading account of W. Wilkins for the month ended 31 May 1984

		£
Sales (950 × £3)		2,850
Opening stock (1 May 1984)	375	
Cost of finished production	2,585	
	2,960	
less Closing stock (200 × £25.85) (1)	517	
Cost of sales		2,443
Gross profit		£407

NOTE

(1) Stock of birdbaths (1 May)	150	
add birdbaths completed	1,000	
	1,150	
less birdbaths sold	950	
Stock at 31 May	200	
Total cost of finished production		£2,585
divided by number of birdbaths completed		1,000
cost per finished birdbath		£2.585

(b)   (i) £2,295

    (ii) £2,685

    (iii) $\dfrac{£2,685}{1,000} = £2.685$ $200 \times £2.685 = £537$

    (iv) £2,523

    (v) £327

19 Stock Valuation

19.1 Introduction

We have already seen that stock is an asset of the business. In all of the examples so far, a closing stock valuation has been given to us in the question. We shall now look closer at how the stock valuation figure is arrived at and the problems involved. We first of all should consider the various bases on which we can value stock.

19.2 Bases of stock valuation

We can summarise the bases as follows:

  (i) Selling price.
  (ii) Net realisable value. This we can define as selling price less costs to be incurred to bring the stock into a saleable condition and then sell it. In other words, selling price less processing costs and selling costs still to be incurred.
 (iii) Original cost.
 (iv) Current replacement cost.

We can ignore (iv), because it is used only in current cost accounting and not conventional historical cost accounting, the latter being the only type with which we are concerned. If we consider the valuation of stock at selling price, this would clearly be unreasonable, since, when we eventually sell the goods, we would make a loss to the extent of processing and selling costs incurred after the stock valuation date. Therefore by valuing stock at selling price we would be recognising a false profit.

Having dismissed (i) and (iv), we are therefore left with the choice of valuing stock at cost or net realisable value. In making the choice between these two bases we must first of all bear in mind accounting convention, which says that stock should be valued at cost until it is sold. In other words, no profit should be recognised until the profit is realised, which is when the sale takes place. Having said that stock should be valued at cost and the profit not recognised until the stock is sold, what if we now consider that we will not be able to sell to stock at a profit? The answer to this problem lies in an accounting concept of prudence. This concept forces us to recognise a loss immediately we are aware of it, and therefore, if the net realisable value of stock is lower than cost, then we should value it at its net realisable value.

If we accept that accounting convention requires us to value stock at the lower of cost and net realisable value, the next question is one of how to apply this basis.

Consider the following example:

Item	Cost	Net realisable value (NRV)	Lower of Cost and NRV
	£	£	£
A	100	150	100
B	600	540	540
C	410	450	410
Total	£1,110	£1,140	£1,050

Can we value the stock at £1,110, since in total the cost of the stock is lower than the net realisable value? The answer is no, we must look separately at each item of stock, although, if this is impracticable, we may look at groups of items and apply the lower of cost or NRV rule to each group of items. In the above example, therefore, stock should be valued at £1,050.

We have mentioned the word 'cost' without defining what cost is, and the different methods of ascertaining cost, which we shall now do.

19.3 Valuation of stocks at cost

You may consider that valuation of stocks at cost is a simple matter, but consider the example of a trader buying and selling cabinets with the following transactions:

Date	Purchases	Sales	Stock remaining
Jan. 1	10 at £15		10
Jan. 21	10 at £17		20
Jan. 27		8	12
Feb. 8	20 at £20		32
Feb. 21		24	8

What is the cost of the 8 cabinets in stock — £15, £17, £20 each, or some other figure? We shall now look at some bases for determining cost and see how it affects the answer to this question.

(a) First in First out (FIFO)

Using this method, we assume that the stock which has been held longest is used first. Therefore, the stock balance represents the latest purchases. In our above example the 8 cabinets would be valued at £20 each.

(b) Last in First out (LIFO)

Using this method, we assume that the stock purchased more recently is used first. Applying this to our example above, we would value the 8 cabinets at £15 each, the explanation being that the 8 sold on 27 January would be from the purchases on 21 January and the 24 sold on 21 February would be as follows:

20 purchased on 8 February
 2 remaining from 21 January purchases
 2 from purchases on 1 January
___
24

Therefore the 8 remaining are from the 10 purchased on 1 January.

(c) Average Cost

Using this method, we calculate the average cost ruling when the stock is sold or used. There are variations in practice but the most common way of applying it to our above example would be as follows:

Date	Purchases	Sales	Stock remaining
Jan. 1	10 × £15 = £150		10 × £15 = 150
Jan. 21	10 × £17 = £170		10 × £15 = 150
			10 × £17 = 170
			20 £320
Jan. 27		(1) 8 × £16 = £128	12 × £16 = £192
Feb. 8	20 × £20 = £400		12 × £16 = £192
			20 × £20 = £400
			32 £592
Feb. 21		(2) 24 × £18.50 = £444	8 × £18.50 = £148

NOTES

(1) The £16 is calculated by dividing the total cost of stock purchased by the quantity purchased (£320 ÷ 20 = £16). £16 is used to value the outgoing stock and the remaining balance.
(2) The £18.50 is calculated by dividing the value of stock in hand by the quantity held at 21 February £592 ÷ 32 = £18.50). Again the £18.50 is used to value the outgoing stock and the balance of stock in hand.

19.4   Choice of method

If we summarise the value using the above three methods, we have

FIFO   8 × £20 = £160
LIFO   8 × £15 = £120
Average   8 × £18.50 = £148

There are other less common methods of valuing stock at cost, but we need not be concerned with those here. Examining the three methods above, we can see that LIFO gives us a lower stock valuation than FIFO, and this will always be the case when prices are rising. Each business is free to choose the method of stock valuation which it considers most appropriate. It is worth noting that FIFO is the most common method and most appropriate in the majority of cases. It also resembles most closely what happens in practice — that is, the oldest stock is sold or used first.

19.5   Effect on profits

It is important that we understand the effect on profits of different stock valuations. Closing stock decreases our cost of sales; therefore, an increase in the closing stock valuation will increase our gross and net profit. Conversely, if we decrease the value of our closing stock, then cost of sales increases and gross and net profits decrease. You should note that the effect will be the opposite when in the next accounting period the closing stock valuation from the previous accounting period becomes the opening stock for the current period. An increase in the opening stock valuation increases cost of sales and therefore decreases gross and net profits. A decrease in opening stock valuation decreases the cost of sales and therefore increases gross and net profits.

19.6 Worked examples

Example 19.1

(a) Explain the meaning of each of the following categories of stock, found in the accounts of a sole trader who manufactures radios:
  (i) stock of finished goods;
  (ii) work in progress;
  (iii) packing materials.
  How would each item be treated in the preparation of final accounts?   [*8 marks*]
(b) "Cost or net realisable value, whichever is the lower". Explain and illustrate the meaning of this statement, which is used in connection with stock valuation.   [*7 marks*]

Solution 19.1

(a) (i) Refer to Section 18.3 (c). Goods ready for sale. Opening stock debited in trading account, included as a plus figure in the cost of sales calculation. Closing stock credited in trading account, included as a minus figure in the cost of sales calculation.
  (ii) Refer to Section 18.3 (b). Partly manufactured goods not yet completed and still being worked on. Opening stock debited in manufacturing account, closing stock credited in manufacturing account.
  (iii) Stock of packing materials purchased but unused. Refer to Section 12.4. Deduct from packing materials expense.
  Note: Additionally all three items of stock will appear as an asset in the balance sheet under current assets.

(b) Refer to Section 19.2.

Example 19.2

The items below have been extracted from the final accounts and balance sheets of the wholesaling business owned by J. White:

	£
Net profit: for 1981	25,600
for 1982	29,240
Gross profit: for 1981	218,450
for 1982	231,620
Stock: 31 December 1981	37,970
31 December 1982	41,810
Capital: 31 December 1981	212,940
31 December 1982	220,650

It has now been discovered that some errors were made at the 31 December 1981 stock-taking: the correct value for stock at that date was £35,250, not £37,970.

You are asked to write out the list of items given above, showing them all at their correct amounts.

(OLE)

Solution 19.2

The decrease in the closing stock valuation at 31 December 1981 will increase cost of sales and therefore decrease gross profit and net profit. Since the net profit is transferred to the capital account, the effect on the balance sheet will be to decrease the capital figure. The asset stock will be decreased similarly, so that the balance sheet balances. We can tabulate the effect as follows:

	Present £	Adjustment £	Revised £
Net profit for 1981	25,600	− 2,720	22,880
Gross profit for 1981	218,450	− 2,720	215,730
Stock 31 December 1981	37,970	+ 2,720	40,690
Capital 31 December 1981	212,940	− 2,720	210,220

In 1982 the reduced opening stock valuation at 1 January 1982 will reduce the cost of sales and therefore increase gross and net profit. Again we can tabulate the effect as follows:

	Present	Adjustment	Revised
Net profit for 1982	29,240	+ 2,720	31,960
Gross profit for 1982	231,620	+ 2,720	234,340
Stock 31 December 1982	41,810	no change	41,810
Capital 31 December 1982		− 2,720 (1981 profit)	220,650 (see below)
	220,650	+ 2,720 (1982 profit)	

In 1981 the balance on the capital account was reduced by £2,720 because of the decreased net profit. The figure brought forward into 1982 would therefore be similarly decreased. However, since the 1982 profit is increased by the same amount of £2,720, the balance on the capital account at 31 December 1982 will be the same as previously.

19.7 Further exercises

Question 19.1

P. Smithers was unable to take stock on 31 December 1981 but carried out the operation on 4 January 1982.

On 4 January 1982 he had the following in stock:

Item no.	Quantity	Cost price per 100 £	Selling price per 100 £
1	4,000	1.10	1.70
2	3,700	1.00	1.40
3	2,000	1.20	1.60
4	1,500	2.10	0.50
5	1,600	2.00	2.40

Smithers points out that the demand for item no. 4 had collapsed and that he was clearing his stock at a very reduced selling price.

Between 1 January 1982 and 4 January 1982 (inclusive) the following had been delivered to P. Smithers' warehouse and had been included in his stock on 4 January:

Item no.	Quantity
2	400
5	300

Sales records shows that the following sales had taken place between 1 January and 4 January 1982:

Item no.	Quantity
1	100
2	200
4	100

(a) Calculate the value of P. Smithers' stock on 31 December 1981.

(b) Why is it important to ascertain stock valuations correctly at the end of a trading period?

(L)

Answer 19.1

(a)

Item	Quantity 4 Jan. 82	Adjustment for Jan. movements	Quantity 31 Dec. 84	Value per 100 (1) £	Stock value £
1	4,000	+ 100	4,100	1.10	45.10
2	3,700	$\left(\begin{array}{c}+200\\-400\end{array}\right)$	3,500	1.00	35.00
3	2,000		2,000	1.20	24.00
4	1,500	+ 100	1,600	0.50	8.00
5	1,600	− 300	1,300	2.00	26.00
					£138.10

NOTE

(1) Lower of cost or net realisable value, in this case the selling price.

(b) Effect on profits of incorrect calculation.

Question 19.2

(a) From the following stock list calculate the value of J. Brown's stock on 31 December 1983.

Item Catalogue number	Quantity in stock	Cost price each £	Selling price each £
1	30	2.40	3.60
2	37	3.10	4.50
3	25	4.20	2.00
4	30	3.70	Nil

(b) A trading account shows the gross profit for three years ended 31 December to be as follows:

	£
1981	16,000
1982	15,000
1983	17,000

It came to light that a quantity of stock, at cost price £400, purchased in 1981 and sold during 1983 had not been included in the stock valuations on 31 December 1981 and 1982.

Calculate the correct gross profit for the three years ended 31 December 1981, 1982 and 1983.

(c) A firm started in business during 1982. On 31 December 1982 stock-taking showed the value of goods held to be £3,700. On 31 December 1983 the value of stock was £4,200. Write up the stock account for the two years 1982 and 1983.

(L)

Answer 19.2

(a)

Item	Quantity	Value (each) (1) £	Stock value £
1	30	2.40	72
2	27	3.10	84
3	25	2.00	50
4	30	Nil	
			£206

NOTE

(1) Lower of cost and net realisable value.

(b)

	As given £	Adjustment £	Revised amount £
1981	16,000	+ 400	16,400
1982	15,000	+ 400	15,000
		− 400	
1983	17,000	− 400	16,600

1981 Closing stock increased; therefore, cost of sales decreased and profits increased.

1982 Opening and closing stocks both undervalued by £400; therefore, no effect on cost of sales or profit.

1983 Opening stock increased by £400; therefore, cost of sales increased and profits decreased.

(c)

Stock

1982		£	1982		£
Dec. 31	Trading account	3,700	Dec. 31	Balance c/d	3,700
		3,700			3,700
1983			1983		
Jan. 1	Balance b/d	3,700	Dec. 31	Trading account	3,700
Dec. 31	Trading account	4,200	Dec. 31	Balance c/d	4,200
		7,900			7,900
1984			1984		
Jan. 1	Balance b/d	4,200			

Question 19.3

(a) Explain the meaning of the following terms, used in connection with stock valuation:
   (i) first in first out (FIFO);
   (ii) last in first out (LIFO). [*5 marks*]

(b) Use an example to show which of the two methods (FIFO or LIFO) will produce a higher figure of stock valuation in times of rising stock prices. [*5 marks*]

(c) Explain the effect on a firm's gross profit of overvaluing closing stock. [*5 marks*]

(AEB)

Answer 19.3

(a) (i) Refer to Section 19.3(a).
    (ii) Refer to Section 19.3(b).

(b) Refer to Sections 19.3 and 19.4.

(c) Refer to Section 19.5.

20 Comprehension and Interpretation of Accounts

20.1 Introduction

We have so far been concerned with the preparation of final accounts without any examination of those accounts and without asking ourselves what those accounts mean or what they are telling us. In order to remedy this situation, we need to calculate some ratios from the figures in the final accounts. In addition to the calculation of ratios, we really need a yardstick or something else with which to compare our figures. For this purpose we may use any or all of the following: (a) previous year's figures; (b) competitors' figures; (c) average figures for the type of business which we are running. We shall now look at some accounting ratios in detail.

20.2 Return on capital employed (ROCE)

This is the most important of ratios which we calculate, since it measures the profit of the business compared with the investment in that business or the capital employed by the business. The formula is

$$\frac{\text{profit}}{\text{capital employed}} \times 100$$

For example,

$$\frac{\pounds15 \text{ (net profit)}}{\pounds200 \text{ (capital employed)}} \times 100 = 7.5 \text{ per cent}$$

Our return on capital employed is 7.5 per cent.

If we wished to improve our ROCE, we could either increase profits or reduce the capital employed, which leads us into our next two sets of ratios.

20.3 Profitability ratios

If in the above example our £15 had been arrived at as follows:

	£
Sales	50
Cost of sales	30
Gross profit	20
Expenses	5
Net profit	£15

We can calculate the following:

(a) Net profit margin, defined as $\dfrac{\text{net profit}}{\text{sales}} \times 100$

as follows: $\dfrac{£15 \text{ (net profit)}}{£50 \text{ (sales)}} \times 100 = 30$ per cent

(b) Gross profit margin, defined as $\dfrac{\text{gross profit}}{\text{sales}} \times 100$

as follows: $\dfrac{£20 \text{ (gross profit)}}{£50 \text{ (sales)}} \times 100 = 40$ per cent

You should be careful not to confuse gross profit margin with mark-up. Margin is the gross profit expressed as a percentage of sales; mark-up is gross profit expressed as a percentage of cost of goods sold. For example, a mark-up of 50 per cent means that if the cost price is £100, the selling price is £100 + £50 — that is, £150. The gross margin in this example is

$$\frac{£50}{£150} \times 100 = 33\tfrac{1}{3} \text{ per cent}$$

20.4 Asset efficiency ratios

As might be expected, the asset efficiency ratio shows how efficient we have been in the use of our assets. The formula is

$$\frac{\text{sales}}{\text{net assets}}$$

Using the same figures as for the previous example, and remembering that if capital employed by the business is £200, then our net assets must also be £200, because of the balance sheet equation referred to in Chapter 4,

$$\frac{£50 \text{ (sales)}}{£200 \text{ (net assets)}} = 0.25$$

The higher the ratio the more efficient we are in using our net assets.

At this stage we should appreciate the relationship referred to in the last paragraph of Section 20.2, which we can now express mathematically as

ROCE = profit margin × asset turnover

or, using the figures from our example used so far,

7.5 per cent = 30 per cent × 0.25

This re-emphasises the point that ROCE depends upon profit margin and asset efficiency.

In considering asset efficiency we should also look at the efficiency of the business with regard to individual assets. We shall now look at two of those assets, stock and debtors.

(a) Stock Turnover

Assets efficiency means keeping the asset figures as low as possible in relation to sales. Stock turnover measures our efficiency in keeping stock as low as possible in relation to sales — that is to say, turning over the stock as many times as possible. The formula is

$$\frac{\text{cost of sales}}{\text{stock}}$$

The stock figure may be average stock or the closing stock. If in the example used so far the closing stock was £12, our stock turnover would be

$$\frac{£30 \text{ (cost of sales)}}{£12 \text{ (stock)}} = 2.5$$

This means that we are turning over our stock $2\frac{1}{2}$ times a year. The higher the stock turnover the more efficient we are.

(b) Debt Collection Period

This measures how efficient we are at keeping our debtors as low as possible in relation to our sales. The formula is

$$\frac{\text{debtors}}{\text{credit sales}} \times 365 = \text{debt collection period, in days}$$

If in the above example our debtors were £8 and all of our sales were on the credit, the calculation would be

$$\frac{£8 \text{ (debtors)}}{£50 \text{ (sales)}} \times 365 = 58 \text{ days}$$

This means that the debtors figure of £8 is equivalent to 58 days of sales, or, put another way, it is taking on average 58 days to collect from our debtors the amounts due from them. The lower the collection period the more efficient we are, both from the point of view of keeping our total assets as low as possible in relation to sales and of reducing the risk of bad debts arising.

20.5 Liquidity ratios

Liquidity ratios measure our ability to be able to finance our day-to-day operations, or, in other words, pay our debts as they become due.

(a) Current Ratio or Working Capital Ratio

The current ratio measures the relationship between current assets and current liabilities by dividing the former by the latter. If the ratio is high, meaning a high level of current assets compared with current liabilities, we should have little difficulty in meeting our debts as they become due.

There are many opinions as to what the ratio should or should not be. Some suggest 2 or even 3 as a rule of thumb, but really it depends on the type of business. Sainsbury's current ratio at 28 March 1984 was 0.49, owing to minimal debtors and low stocks, but this cannot be interpreted as indicating any financial instability. In the case of the current ratio, it is important to look at how the figure has changed when compared with the previous year rather than the figure itself. A decrease compared with the previous year would be a warning sign as to the financial stability of the business. Finally, we should not fail to note that while a high current ratio denotes strong financial stability, it may also indicate poor asset efficiency.

(b) Acid Test Ratio

The formula for the acid test ratio is

$$\frac{\text{current assets (less stock)}}{\text{current liabilities}}$$

Like the current ratio, it measures liquidity but is less commonly used. The same comments apply with regard to meaning and interpretation as to the current ratio.

20.6 Worked examples

Example 20.1

(a) The following figures, in £000s, relate to two similar businesses, X and Y.

	X	Y
	£000s	£000s
Turnover	18,000	24,000
Capital	15,000	16,800
Net profit	1,800	3,360
Gross profit	4,500	6,000
Average stock at cost	1,500	1,500

Calculate for businesses X and Y:
 (i) net profit percentage on capital;
 (ii) net profit percentage on sales;
 (iii) gross profit percentage on sales;
 (iv) rate of stock turnover.

(b) A financial magazine publishes an article claiming the following figures should be the norm for a well-run business:

Net profit on capital	15 per cent
Net profit on sales	12 per cent
Gross profit on sales	25 per cent
Rate of stock turnover	10

Compare the relationships which you have calculated in (a) with the published norm and state, with reasons, which business is the better managed.

(L)

Solution 20.1

(a)

	X	Y

(i) $\dfrac{1,800}{15,000} \times 100 = 12$ per cent $\dfrac{3,360}{16,800} \times 100 = 20$ per cent

(ii) $\dfrac{1,800}{18,000} \times 100 = 10$ per cent $\dfrac{3,360}{24,000} \times 100 = 14$ per cent

(iii) $\dfrac{4,500}{18,000} \times 100 = 25$ per cent $\qquad \dfrac{6,000}{24,000} \times 100 = 25$ per cent

(iv) $\dfrac{13,500}{1,500} = 9$ times $\qquad \dfrac{18,000}{1,500} = 12$ times

(b) Y is making a better return on capital employed (20 per cent compared with X's 12 per cent and a norm of 15 per cent). This is partly due to Y making a better net profit margin (14 per cent compared with X's 10 per cent and a norm of 12 per cent). Since both X and Y are making a gross profit margin of 25 per cent (in line with the norm), Y is incurring a lower level of overhead expenses compared with sales than X. The other reason for Y's better net profit margin is asset efficiency, as shown by an asset turnover of 1.43 compared with X's 1.2. One of the reasons for this is Y's ability to turn over his stock 12 times per year compared with a norm of 10 and X's 9. Y is therefore the better-managed business, with net profit margin and stock turnover being better than for X and the norm. This results in a better return on capital employed.

Example 20.2

The trading and profit and loss accounts of two separate businesses, engaged in the same trade and of similar size, are given below.

Trading and Profit and Loss Accounts for year ended 31 December 1983:

	CORFU Ltd £	RHODES Ltd £		CORFU Ltd £	RHODES Ltd £
Opening Stock	2,600	5,300	Sales	48,900	43,500
Purchases	?	?	Less Returns	900	250
	?	?			
Less Closing Stock	?	4,700			
Cost of goods sold	?	?			
Gross Profit	?	?			
	?	?		?	?
Total Expenses	?	?	Gross Profit	?	?
Net Profit	6,000	2,500			
	?	?		?	?

Additional information:

	CORFU Ltd	RHODES Ltd
Capital employed	£20,000	£20,000
Rate of turnover of stock	16	not given
Mark up on cost	50 per cent	25 per cent

REQUIRED

(a) A copy of the above trading and profit and loss accounts, including all the missing figures denoted by question marks. [8 marks]

(b) Calculations for each business of
  (i) gross profit expressed as a percentage of net sales:
  (ii) net profit expressed as a percentage of net sales:
  (iii) return on capital employed. [5 marks]

(c) Consider the information given above and the figures you have calculated and give two reasons why you feel one of the businesses produced a better performance than the other, during the period concerned. [3 marks]

175

(d) Give two other bases of comparison that are frequently used to evaluate the performance of a business. [*1 mark*]

(AEB)

Solution 20.2

(a)

		Corfu Ltd £	Rhodes Ltd £			Corfu Ltd £	Rhodes Ltd £
Opening stock		2,600	5,300	Sales		48,900	43,500
Purchases	(7)	31,000	34,000	less Returns		900	250
	(6)	34,000	39,300				
less Closing stock	(5)	2,000	4,700				
Cost of goods sold	(4)	32,000	34,600				
Gross profit	(3)	16,000	8,650				
	(2)	48,000	43,250		(1)	48,000	43,250
Total expenses	(8)	10,000	6,150	Gross profit	(3)	16,000	8,650
Net Profit		6,000	2,500				
		16,000	8,650			16,000	8,650

NOTES

(1) Sales = sales less returns.
(2) Debit side = credit side of trading account.
(3) Corfu Ltd mark-up on cost 50 per cent; therefore, gross profit margin $33\frac{1}{3}$ per cent of sales or $33\frac{1}{3}$ per cent × £48,000 = £16,000. Rhodes Ltd mark-up on cost 25 per cent; therefore, gross profit margin 20 per cent of sales or 20 per cent × £43,250 = £8,650.
(4) Cost of goods sold = sales less gross profit.
(5) Corfu stock turnover 16; therefore closing stock is cost of goods sold divided by 16 — that is £32,000 ÷ 16 = 2,000.
(6) Cost of goods sold plus closing stock.
(7) Line (6) less opening stock.
(8) Gross profit less net profit.

(b)

	Corfu Ltd	Rhodes Ltd
(i)	$\frac{16,000}{48,000} \times 100 = 33\frac{1}{3}$ per cent	$\frac{8,650}{43,250} \times 100 = 20$ per cent
(ii)	$\frac{6,000}{48,000} \times 100 = 12.5$ per cent	$\frac{2,500}{43,250} \times 100 = 5.8$ per cent
(iii)	$\frac{6,000}{20,000} \times 100 = 30$ per cent	$\frac{2,500}{20,000} \times 100 = 12.5$ per cent

(c) Corfu Ltd's gross profit margin is higher and therefore it could be selling at higher prices than Rhodes Ltd or buying at lower prices. Corfu Ltd is incurring a higher level of expenses and therefore could be paying more for rent, rates, wages or any other item of overhead.

20.7 Further exercises

Question 20.1

P. Farrell is a wholesaler. The following information is available from his accounts for year ended 31 December 1981.

	£
Stock at 31 December 1981	2,990
Purchases	22,254
Sales	30,260
Returns inward	140
Returns outward	210

Mark up: 50 per cent on cost

In the following year Farrell's closing stock was 10 per cent higher than the corresponding figure for 1981 but the rate per cent of gross profit on sales was the same for 1982 as in 1981. In 1982 net sales increased by 10 per cent on the previous year's figure.

REQUIRED

(a) Preparation of Farrell's trading account for year ended 31 December 1981, showing the value of stock at 1 January 1981. [6 marks]
(b) Preparation of Farrell's trading account for year ended 31 December 1982, showing the value of purchases. (There were no returns outward.) [7 marks]
(c) Calculation of the amount of profit and loss account expense items (to the nearest £) which would give a net profit to sales ratio of 15 per cent for year ended 31 December 1982. [4 marks]
(d) An explanation of the effect on a firm's net profit of undervaluing closing stock. [3 marks]

(AEB)

Answer 20.1

(a)
Trading accounts of P. Farrell

	Year ending 31 Dec. 1981		Year ending 31 Dec. 1982	
		£		£
Sales (less returns inwards)		30,120		(6) 33,132
Opening stock	(4) 1,026		(9) 2,990	
Purchases (less returns outward)	22,044		(11) 22,387	
	(3) 23,070		(10) 25,377	
less Closing stock	2,990		(5) 3,289	
Cost of sales		(2) 20,080		(8) 22,088
Gross profit		(1) 10,040		(7) 11,044

WORKINGS

(1) Gross profit mark-up 50 per cent; therefore, margin $33\frac{1}{3}$ per cent. Gross profit therefore $33\frac{1}{3}$ per cent $\times$ £30,120 = £10,040.
(2) Sales less gross profit.
(3) Cost of sales plus closing stock.
(4) Line (3) less purchases.
(5) £2,990 plus 10 per cent.
(6) £30,120 plus 10 per cent.

(7) As for (1): $33\frac{1}{3}$ per cent × £33,132

(8) As for (2).

(9) Closing stock at 31 December 1981.

(10) As for (3).

(11) Line (10) less line (9).

(c)

	1981 £	1982 £
Net profit	4,518	4,970
Expenses (gross profit less net profit)	5,522	6,074

(d) Closing stock decreases cost of sales and therefore increases profit. Refer to Chapter 19.

Question 20.2

The following is the Trial Balance of E. Bowie AFTER he has calculated his Gross Profit for the year ending 31 March 1984.

Trial Balance of E. Bowie as at 31 March 1984

	£	£
Gross Profit		25,600
Debtors and Creditors		11,900
Drawings	7,300	
Selling and Administrative Expenses	11,100	
Provision for Doubtful Debts		800
Premises at cost	62,000	
Motor Vehicles at cost	18,600	
Fixtures and fittings at cost	8,400	
Provisions for Depreciation		
Premises		16,400
Motor Vehicles		6,600
Fixtures and Fittings		2,360
Stock 31 March 1984	14,640	
Cash Balance	1,420	
Bank Balance		5,800
Capital Account		70,290
	£139,750	£139,750

STUDY the above Trial Balance, then answer the following questions:

(a) Calculate the COST OF GOODS SOLD if the rate of gross profit to sales is 20 per cent.   *3*

(b) Calculate the PERCENTAGE MARK-UP (gross profit on cost of goods sold).   *2*

(c) Calculate the PURCHASES for year ending 31 March 1984 if the stock on 31 March 1983 was valued at £15,360.   *3*

(d) (i) HOW does the Provision for Depreciation on Motor Vehicles (as shown in the Trial Balance) help to provide for the eventual replacement of the Motor Vehicles?   *3*

    (ii) Give ONE REASON why this aim (in part (d) (i)) may not always be achieved.   *1*

(e) Calculate the RATE OF STOCK TURNOVER for the year ending 31 March 1984 (giving your answer to one decimal place).   *3*

                                                                     (*15*)

Answer 20.2

(a) Sales = £25,600 × $\dfrac{100}{20}$ = £128,000

(b) $\dfrac{£25,600}{(£128,000 - £25,600)}$ × 100 = 25 per cent

	£
(c) Opening stock	15,360
Purchases (balancing figure)	101,680
	117,040
Closing stock	14,640
Cost of goods sold	£102,400

(d) (i) Refer to Chapter 11.
    (ii) Inflation.

(e) $\dfrac{£102,400}{£14,640}$ = 7.0 times, using closing stock method

or

$\dfrac{£102,400}{£15,000}$ = 6.8 times, using average stock method.

21 Accounts of Limited Companies

21.1 Introduction

The format of the final accounts of limited companies is laid down in the Companies Act 1985. We need not concern ourselves at this level with a detailed study of the published formats, but you should carefully study the worked examples and follow the format which is used there in answering questions on accounts of limited companies. First of all, what is a limited company and what does 'limited' refer to? The answer is that the owner's liability is limited to the capital of the business. In the case of sole traders and partnerships, if the business runs up debts, the proprietor is responsible for those debts and his personal assets can be taken in order to pay them. This is not so with a limited company. Outsiders are therefore more willing to invest in such a company than in a partnership, because they know the maximum amount which they can lose – i.e. the nominal value (explained later) of the shares they agree to buy.

21.2 Share capital

The owner's capital in a limited company consists of share capital. When a company commences, it issues shares to investors, who then become shareholders. These shares are denominated in units of monetary value – for example, 25p or £1. This value is called the nominal value. When discussing share capital, we must be careful to distinguish between the following:

(i) Authorised capital is the maximum amount of share capital that a company is empowered to issue by its constitution. It must appear by way of note on the balance sheet.

(ii) Issued capital is the amount of a company's authorised share capital that it has actually issued. A company will not normally issue all of its authorised share capital when it commences, but will wait until it needs additional funds. Provided that all of the issued shares have been paid for in full, it is the nominal value of the issued share capital which will appear on the balance sheet.

(iii) Preference shares carry the right to a fixed dividend (explained later) before any dividend can be paid to other shareholders.

(iv) Ordinary shares are the most common type of shares and carry no right to a fixed dividend, but are entitled to all profits after payment of dividends to preference shareholders. Effectively, it is the ordinary shareholders who control a company, since they have the right to vote at meetings.

21.3   Debentures

Simply stated, debentures are loans to a company. The company pays interest on the loans to the debenture holders. Interest is an expense of the company, just like any other expense such as wages and rent. If the interest is paid in arrears and is outstanding at the balance sheet date, we must accrue for it in the same way as we accrue for any other unpaid expense. In the worked examples you should notice how debentures are deducted from the net assets of the company and not shown with capital.

21.4   Dividends

Assuming that a company makes a profit it has the choice between (a) paying out the profits to shareholders, which is called a dividend, and (b) retaining the profits in the company to finance investment in additional assets.

Dividends are an appropriation of profit and are usually paid in two stages:

(i) Interim dividend, paid when the half-year results or profits are known.
(ii) Final dividend, usually paid after the end of the year, when the profit for the year is known. Dividends are expressed as a percentage of the nominal value of the shares.

Both dividends must be shown as an appropriation of profit in the profit and loss account, whether paid or unpaid. To the extent that they are unpaid, they must be shown as a current liability in the balance sheet. Often the unpaid dividends are referred to as proposed dividends.

21.5   Retained profits

The balance which remains on the profit and loss account after deducting dividends is referred to as profit and loss account balance, retained earnings, retained profits or undistributed profits. All of these terms mean the same, and we shall now consider the accounting treatment.

In the case of the sole trader, the profit and loss account is closed by transferring the balance to the owner's capital account. In the case of a company, the balance remains on the profit and loss account, which means that it appears on the balance sheet and is carried forward to the next year. The profit and loss account balance shown on the balance sheet will therefore represent retained earnings (which is profit less dividends) in respect of all previous years.

We also refer to retained earnings as part of the reserves of the company, since it represents profits held back and not distributed as dividends. In using the word 'reserve' we must not think that there is cash in the business of that amount; there usually will not be. As we stated previously, those retained profits are used to purchase fixed assets and finance working capital requirements.

21.6   General reserve

Sometimes a company prefers not to show a large profit and loss account balance on its balance sheet. The reason is that it may be misconstrued as representing a cash surplus which is available for distribution as dividends. To overcome this, we transfer an amount from our profit and loss account to a general reserve account. The transfer to reserve is shown as an appropriation of profit on the profit and loss account (explained in Section 21.8) and the balance on the general reserve account is shown on the balance sheet.

21.7 Shareholders' funds

This term is used to describe the share capital and reserves of the business. The two examples of reserves that we have met so far are profit and loss account and general reserve account. Shareholders' funds therefore represents the shareholders' investment in the company.

21.8 Profit and loss appropriation account

This account performs much the same function in companies' books as with a partnership. It commences with the net profit of the business and shows appropriations of profit by way of dividends (paid and proposed) and transfers to general reserve. The account will also be credited with the balance brought forward from the previous accounting period, representing undistributed profits from previous years.

21.9 Worked examples

Example 21.1

John Arnold is the owner of 25,000 ordinary shares in Arnold Ltd. His wife, Pauline, is the only other shareholder, owning 5,000 ordinary shares. The business is a small firm engaged in the manufacture of footwear. In order to reduce accountancy charges, Mr Arnold decided to prepare the final accounts himself. However, he did not meet with complete success, as can be seen from an examination of his balance sheet, at 31 December 1982, given below.

Balance Sheet of Arnold Limited for period ended 31 December 1982

Liabilities		Assets	
35,000 £1 Ordinary shares		Premises at cost	25,000
(Auth. Cap.)	35,000	Machinery and plant at cost	10,500
Net profit for 1982	2,865	Stock of finished goods at	
Profit and loss balance		31 December 1982	960
1 January 1982	6,230	Stock of raw materials at	
Provision for depreciation on		31 December 1982	3,270
machinery and plant	5,500	Cash	528
Provision for bad debts	90	Debtors	2,800
Stock of work in progress at		Electricity accrued	66
31 December 1982	2,900	Income receivable	692
Creditors	899		
Bank loan (to be repaid in 1985)	1,000		
	54,484		43,816

Mr Arnold is certain that all figures given above are correct. However, he feels that some of the items may be incorrectly classified. A dividend of £3,000 is proposed for 1982.

REQUIRED

(a) (i) Preparation of the profit and loss appropriation account for the year ended 31 December 1982. [2 marks]

(ii) Preparation of the balance sheet in good form distinguishing between fixed and current assets. Show within the balance sheet the value of authorised and issued capital, working capital, reserves and shareholders' funds. [15 marks]

(b) An explanation of the meaning of (i) "authorised capital",
(ii) "issued capital". [3 marks]

(AEB)

Solution 21.1

(a) (i)

Profit and loss appropriation account of Arnold Ltd for year ended 31 December 1982

	£
Net profit for the year	2,865
add Profit and loss account balance as at the beginning of the year	6,230
	9,095
less Proposed dividends	3,000
Profit and loss account balance as at the end of the year	**£6,095**

(ii)
Balance sheet of Arnold Ltd at 31 December 1982

Fixed Assets	Cost	Depreciation	Net book value
	£	£	£
Premises	25,000		25,000
Machinery and plant	10,500	5,500	5,000
	35,500	5,500	30,000

Current Assets				
Stock — raw materials	3,270			
— work in progress	2,900			
— finished goods	960	7,130		
Debtors	2,800			
less provision for bad debts	90	2,710		
Accrued income		692		
Cash		528		
		11,060		
less Creditors: amounts falling due within one year (1)				
Creditors	899			
Accrued expenses	66			
Proposed dividends	3,000	3,965		
Net Current Assets (or working capital)			7,095	
Net Assets			37,095	
less Creditors: amounts falling due after more than one year (2)				
Bank loan			1,000	
			£36,095	

Shareholders' Funds

Authorised share capital (35,000 £1 ordinary shares)   £35,000

Issued share capital — ordinary shares   30,000
Reserves — Profit and loss account   6,095
                                                                 £36,095

NOTES

(1), (2) You should note all terms used but in particular how current liabilities and other liabilities are described in company accounts.

(b) (i) Refer to Section 21.2(a).
     (ii) Refer to Section 21.2(b).

Example 21.2

The Green Meadow Cleaning Company is registered with an authorised capital of £25,000,000 divided into 5,000,000 10 per cent preference shares of £1 each and 20,000,000 ordinary shares of £1 each.

The following trial balance was extracted from the company's books on 31 December 1983.

	£000s		£000s
Premises	20,000	Preference capital	5,000
Machinery	4,000	Ordinary capital	15,000
Motor vans	100	Profit and loss	10
Electric power	10,300	12 per cent debentures	1,000
Wages	26,000	Provision for depreciation:	
Heat and light	1,500	Machinery	600
Cleaning materials	400	Vans	20
Rates	700	Creditors	15
Van expenses	50	Receipts for cleaning	42,318
Bank	902		
Cash	11		
	63,963		63,963

Prepare an account to show the cleaning company's profit or loss for the year ended 31 December 1983, and a Balance Sheet on that date before the appropriation account is prepared and dividends declared or paid.

Take into consideration the following:

	£000s
(i) Rates paid in advance	140
(ii) Heat and light account unpaid	7
(iii) Provision for depreciation of machinery to be increased to	900
(iv) Provision for depreciation of motor vans to be increased to	70
(v) Provision for the debenture interest	120

184

Solution 21.2

Profit and loss account of The Green Meadow Cleaning Company for the year ended 31 December 1983

			£000
Turnover			42,318
less Wages		26,000	
Other operating charges			
Electric power	10,300		
Heat and light (£1,500 + £7)	1,507		
Cleaning materials	400		
Rates (£700 − £140)	560		
Van expenses	50		
Depreciation machinery	300		
Depreciation motor vans	50	13,167	39,167
			3,151
less Interest payable			120
Net profit for the year			£3,031

Balance sheet of The Green Meadow Cleaning Company as at 31 December 1983

Fixed Assets	Cost	Depreciation	Net book value
	£	£	£
Premises	20,000		20,000
Machinery	4,000	900	3,100
Motor vans	100	70	30
	24,100	970	23,130

Current Assets			
Prepayments		140	
Cash at bank and in hand		913	
		1,053	

less Creditors: amounts falling due within 1 year

Creditors	15		
Accrued expenses (£120 + £7)	127	142	

Net Current Assets (or working capital)			911
Net Assets			24,041
less Creditors: amounts falling due after more than 1 year			
12 per cent debentures			1,000
			£23,041

Shareholders' Funds

Authorised share capital		
5,000,000 10 per cent preference shares of £1	5,000	
20,000,000 ordinary shares of £1	20,000	
	25,000	

Issued share capital		
5,000,000 10 per cent preference shares of £1		5,000
15,000,000 ordinary shares of £1		15,000
		20,000

Reserves − profit and loss account		
− balance brought forward	10	
− add net profit for the year	3,031	3,041
		£23,041

21.10 Further exercises

Question 21.1

Ogden Limited had an authorised capital of £100,000, divided into 75,000 ordinary shares of £1 each and 25,000 8 per cent preference shares of £1 each. The following balances remained in the account of the company after the trading and profit and loss accounts had been prepared for the year ended 31 December 1982.

	Debit £	Credit £
Ordinary share capital: fully paid		50,000
8 per cent preference shares: fully paid		15,000
Machinery and plant at cost	40,000	
Provision for depreciation on machinery and plant		19,000
Premises at cost	50,000	
Profit and loss account balance (1 January 1982)		5,600
Net profit (for year ended 31 December 1982)		9,026
Light and heat		280
Cash at bank	3,508	
Stock	3,860	
Debtors and Creditors	2,300	894
Insurance	132	
	99,800	99,800

The directors have recommended an ordinary dividend of 12 per cent and wish to provide for payment of the year's preference share dividend.

REQUIRED

(a) The profit and loss appropriation account for year ended 31 December 1982   [*3 marks*]
(b) The balance sheet as at 31 December 1982, in a form which shows clearly the shareholders' funds and the working capital.   [*13 marks*]
(c) An explanation of the term "limited liability".   [*1 mark*]
(d) A statement of three differences between an ordinary share and a debenture.   [*3 marks*]

(AEB)

Answer 21.1

(a)

Profit and loss appropriation account of Ogden Ltd for the year ended 31 December 1982

		£
Net profit for the year		9,026
add Profit and loss account balance as at the beginning of the year		5,600
		14,626
less Dividends — preference shares	1,200	
— ordinary shares	6,000	7,200
Profit and loss account balance as at end of year		£7,426

186

(b)
Balance sheet of Ogden Ltd as at 31 December 1982

Fixed Assets	Cost	Depreciation	Net book value
	£	£	£
Premises	50,000		50,000
Plant and machinery	40,000	19,000	21,000
	90,000	19,000	71,000

Current Assets		
Stock	3,860	
Debtors	2,300	
Prepayments	132	
Cash at bank	3,508	
	9,800	

less Creditors: amounts falling due within 1 year

Creditors	894	
Dividends	7,200	
Expense creditors	280	8,374

Net Current Assets (or working capital)	1,426
Net Assets	£72,426

Shareholders' Funds
Authorised share capital

75,000 £1 Ordinary shares	75,000
25,000 £1 8 per cent Preference shares	25,000
	100,000

Issued share capital

50,000 £1 Ordinary Shares	50,000
15,000 £1 8 per cent Preference shares	15,000
	65,000
Reserves — profit and loss account	7,426
	£72,426

(c) Refer to Section 12.1.

(d) Debentures are loans to the company; ordinary shares are an investment in the company. Debenture holders are creditors of the company, not shareholders. Debentures are usually repayable, and as loans have preference for repayment over shareholders in the event of a winding up. Interest is payable on debentures and must be paid irrespective of whether profits are made, whereas ordinary shareholders earn dividends, which are only payable if profits are made. Interest is an expense of the company; dividends are an appropriation of profit.

Question 21.2

The Polite Company Ltd is registered with an authorised capital of £850,000 divided into 250,000 10% preference shares of £1 each and 600,000 ordinary shares of £1 each.

The following balances remain in the books after completion of trading, profit and loss accounts for the year ended 31 March 1985.

	£000
Ordinary capital	550
Preference capital	250
Land and buildings	800
Provisions for depreciation	
Fixtures and fittings	100
Motor vehicles	80
Fixtures and fittings	220
Motor vehicles	120
Creditors	20
Profit and loss (Cr) b/f	5
Trading profit for year	100
Stocks	70
Debtors	15
Debentures 7%	100
Bank overdraft	23
Cash in hand	3

The directors propose to pay the preference dividend and a dividend of 12% on the ordinary shares.

(a) Prepare a profit and loss appropriation account and a Balance Sheet on that date showing the effect of these proposals. [21 marks]

(b) Comment on the liquidity position of the company if the dividends are paid. [3 marks]

(L)

Answer 21.2

(a)

Polite Company Ltd Profit and loss appropriation account for the year ended 31 March 1985

		£000s
Trading profit		100
Dividends: preference	25	
ordinary	72	97
Retained profit for the year		3
Retained profits b/f		5
Retained profits c/f		8

Polite Company Ltd Balance sheet as at 31 March 1985

Fixed Assets	Cost	Depreciation	£000s Net book value
Land and buildings	800	–	800
Fixtures and fittings	220	100	120
Motor vehicles	120	80	40
	1,140	180	960

Current Assets		
Stock		70
Debtors		15
Cash in hand		3
		88

less Creditors: amounts falling due within one year

Creditors	20	
Dividends payable	97	
Bank overdraft	23	140

Net Current Assets		(52)
Net Assets		908
less Creditors: amounts falling due after more than one year		
Debentures		100
		£808

Capital and Reserves

Authorised share capital		
600,000 Ordinary shares of £1	600	
250,000 10% Preference shares of £1	250	
	850	
Issued share capital		
550,000 Ordinary shares of £1		550
250,000 10% Preference shares of £1		250
Profit and loss account		8
		£808

(b) The company clearly has insufficient resources to pay the proposed dividends. The creditors falling due within one year of £140,000 are substantially in excess of current assets at £88,000. The dividend policy should therefore be reviewed in order to avoid increasing the existing bank overdraft of £23,000, even if the bank is prepared to allow the increase.

22 Forecasts and Budgets

22.1 Introduction

The object of going into business is to make a profit. But how do we ensure that we achieve that objective? The answer is that we must plan what we are going to do. If we plan what we are going to do, we can set out that plan in figures. The profit and loss accounts prepared in the examples so far have told us historically how much profit or loss we have made. In planning we prepare profit and loss accounts and balance sheets for future periods of time. If we then examine our plans or forecasts we can take any of the following actions:

   (i) Accept the plan as giving us a satisfactory profit and make business decisions based upon that plan.

 (ii) Amend the plan because we consider the profit inadequate.

(iii) Scrap the plan completely and start on fresh plans.

In addition to helping us to achieve a satisfactory profit, planning also helps us to establish whether we have sufficient resources to implement that plan. One important resource will be finance, and our plan will tell us whether we have sufficient financial resources to implement the plan and achieve our required profit.

22.2 Preparation of plans

In preparing forecasts or estimates of future profits, we prepare trading and profit and loss accounts in similar format to our historic accounts in previous chapters. We may, however, require a different approach where we are given the profit that a business is required to make. In this case, instead of commencing with our sales figures and deducting costs to arrive at our profit, we must work in reverse. That is to say, we commence with our net profit and add on our costs to arrive at a sales figure required to achieve the given profit.

22.3 Worked examples

Example 22.1

Mike Baldwin began business as a manufacturer of pocket calculators on 1 April 1983, with a cash capital of £100,000. For the first year the target production is 42,000 calculators and target sales 40,000. The following additional forecasts have been made:

raw materials £2 per unit;
direct labour £1.50 per unit;
variable factory expenses 30p per unit;
variable selling expenses 10p per unit;

fixed factory expenses £8,400;
fixed selling expenses £6,000.

Stock at 31 March 1984: 2,000 calculators valued at factory cost.

The selling price is to be determined by adding 25 per cent to the factory cost of finished output.

REQUIRED

(a) For the year ended 31 March 1984,
    (i) the forecast manufacturing account, showing clearly the prime cost and the factory cost of goods manufactured;   [6 marks]
    (ii) your calculation of the factory cost per calculator: [1 mark]
    (iii) the forecast trading and profit and loss accounts, showing clearly the factory cost of the goods sold.   [7 marks]

(b) (i) An explanation of the meaning of variable expense and fixed expense;   [2 marks]
    (ii) a statement of the significance to a business of distinguishing between fixed and variable expenses.   [2 marks]

(AEB)

Solution 22.1

(a) (i)

Forecast manufacturing account of M. Baldwin for the year ending 31 March 1984

	£
Raw materials	
42,000 at £2 per unit	84,000
Wages	
42,000 at £1.50 per unit	63,000
Direct expenses (1)	
42,000 at 30p per unit	12,600
Prime Cost	159,600
Factory Overheads	8,400
Factory cost of goods manufactured	£168,000

NOTE

(1) Variable expenses have been assumed to be direct.

(ii) Factory cost per calculator:

$$\frac{£168,000}{42,000} = £4 \text{ per calculator}$$

(iii)

Forecast trading and profit and loss account for M. Baldwin for the year ending 31 March 1984

	£	£
Sales (40,000 × (£4 + 25 per cent))		200,000
Cost of goods manufactured	168,000	
less Closing stock (2,000 × £4)	8,000	
Factory cost of goods sold		160,000
Gross profit		40,000

less		
Variable selling expenses (40,000 × 10p)	4,000	
Fixed selling expenses	6,000	10,000
Net profit		£30,000

(b) (i) Refer to Section 18.6. Variable costs vary with number of goods produced, fixed remain at the same total amount for a period of time regardless of the number of units produced.

(ii) Fixed costs will be incurred regardless of the quantity of units produced and therefore the margin between selling price and variable cost per unit must be sufficient to cover fixed costs before a profit is earned.

Example 22.2

D. Bell is a retailer. The following is a summary of his store's trading results for the latest financial year:

	£
Sales	120,000
Cost of goods sold	90,000
Gross profit	30,000
Running expenses	17,600
Net profit	12,400

He is thinking of opening a second store in a new shopping centre, in the same line of business and adopting the same pricing policy. The following information about the proposed new store is available:

(a) Bell will need to borrow £48,000, paying interest at 14 per cent per annum.
(b) He will have to pay £4,400 per annum for assistants' wages.
(c) Rent and rates will cost £2,460 per annum.
(d) Other fixed expenses will amount to £1,000 per annum.
(e) Variable expenses are estimated according to turnover, as follows:

Sales	Variable expenses
	£
Up to £40,000	1,200
£40,000–£60,000	1,400
£60,000–£80,000	1,600
£80,000–£100,000	1,800
£100,000–£120,000	2,000

(f) Bell will require a clear profit of £6,000 per annum from the new store.

You are asked:

(1) to calculate what level of sales must be achieved in order to reach the required level of profit;
(2) to prepare estimated accounts for the new store showing the gross and net profit in its first year, assuming the level of sales calculated in (1) is achieved.

[18]
(OLE)

Solution 22.2

(1) The fixed costs which have to be covered will be as follows:

	£
Interest (£48,000 × 14 per cent)	6,720
Wages	4,400
Rent and rates	2,460
Other	1,000
	14,580
In addition, a profit is required of	6,000
Contribution required to fixed costs and profit	£20,580

We can calculate that Bell's gross profit margin is 25 per cent $\left(\frac{30,000}{120,000}\right)$. Therefore the sales figure required is

$$\frac{100}{25} \times £20,580 = \qquad 82,320$$

Additionally, we must cover variable expenses $\frac{100}{25} \times £1,800$ $\quad$ 7,200

$$£89,520$$

(2) Estimated trading and profit and loss account of D. Bell's new store for first year of trading

		£
Sales		89,520
Cost of goods sold (75 per cent × £89,520)		67,140
Gross profit		22,380
less		
Variable expenses	1,800	
Fixed expenses (as (1) above)	14,580	16,380
		£6,000

22.4 Further exercises

Question 22.1

Juan Thomas has decided to trade as a retailer from 1 February 1986 with £50,000 capital, which he will pay into a business bank account. He has prepared the following forecast for the first year.

		£
Expenses for the year:	rates	650
	sales assistants' wages	9,200
	sundry expenses	1,500
	depreciation on fixed assets	1,800

Net profit will be £10,000.

		£
Items to be purchased in February 1986:	premises	25,000
	delivery van	6,200

Thomas will withdraw £650 per month from the business for his own use.
Selling price will be determined by marking up 50% on cost.
Closing stock at 31 January 1987, valued at cost price, will be £10,000.

All receipts and payments will be through the firm's bank account.

At year end, there will be no trade debtors or trade creditors and no expenses will be prepaid or in arrears.

REQUIRED

    (a) For the year ended 31 January 1987,

        (i) a forecast trading and profit and loss account, incorporating your calculation of cost of goods sold, purchases and sales;   [9 marks]

        (ii) a forecast bank account.   [6 marks]

    (b) **Two** reasons why firms prepare forecast accounts.   [3 marks]

    (c) The effect on the balance sheet of the owner withdrawing goods from the business for private use, cost price £500.   [2 marks]

                                    (AEB)

Answer 22.1

(a)

(i) Juan Thomas forecast trading and profit and loss account for year ending 31 January 1987

		£
Sales (1)		69,450
Purchases (2)	56,300	
less Closing stock	10,000	
Cost of sales		46,300
Gross profit		23,150
less Rates	650	
Wages	9,200	
Sundry	1,500	
Depreciation	1,800	13,150
Net profit		£10,000

WORKINGS

(1) Sales figure will be the total of net profit, overheads and cost of sales as follows:

Net profit		10,000
Expenses: rates	650	
wages	9,200	
sundry	1,500	
depreciation	1,800	13,150
Gross profit		23,150

Sales $\frac{150}{50} \times £23,150 =$ £69,450

(2) Purchases will be the total of cost of sales and closing stock:

Cost of sales (£69,450 − £23,150) =	46,300
Closing stock	10,000
	£56,300

(ii) Forecast bank account

1986			1987		
Feb. 1	Capital	50,000	Jan. 31	Rates	650
1987			Jan. 31	Wages	9,200
Jan. 31	Sales	69,450	Jan. 31	Sundry	1,500
			Jan. 31	Premises	25,000
			Jan. 31	Van	6,200
			Jan. 31	Drawings	7,800

		Jan. 31	Purchases	56,300
		Jan. 31	Balance c/d	12,800
	119,450			£119,450
Feb. 1 Balance b/d	£12,800			

(b) Refer to Section 22.1.
    (i) To formulate business plan.
    (ii) To ensure we have sufficient resources.
(c) Reduce both closing stock and owner's capital account.

Question 22.2

The final accounts for J. Berry's business covering the year ended 31 October 1983 are summarised below:

		£
Sales		180,000
less cost of goods sold:		
Opening stock	27,000	
Purchases	124,000	
	151,000	
Closing stock	31,000	120,000
Gross profit		60,000
Running expenses		25,600
Net profit		34,400

Mr Berry was disappointed with the level of net profit and decided that for the next year's trading the rate of mark-up would be reduced to 40 per cent on cost. He estimated that, as a result, the volume of sales would increase by one-third (i.e. he would, in effect, sell four articles for every three sold in the year ended 31 October 1983).

Mr Berry decided to reduce his stock to £30,000 by 31 October 1984. He expected his running expenses for the year ending 31 October 1984 to be 5 per cent higher than the previous year's figure.

You are asked to prepare estimated final accounts for the year ended 31 October 1984, assuming that all Mr Berry's expectations are realised. Your working must be shown. [*18*]

(OLE)

Answer 22.2

Estimated trading and profit and loss account of J. Berry for the year ending 31 October 1984

		£
Sales (Working 1)		224,000
Opening stock	31,000	
Purchases (Working 3)	159,000	
	190,000	
less Closing stock	30,000	
Cost of sales (Working 2)		160,000
Gross profit		64,000
Running expenses (£25,600 × 105 per cent)		26,880
Net profit		£37,120

195

The mark-up on cost for year ended 31 October 1983 was 50 per cent — that is, $\left(\dfrac{£60,000}{120,000} \times 100\right)$. The mark-up for year ending 31 October 1984 will be 40 per cent. Therefore, goods costing £100 will sell for £140 in year ending 31 October 1984 compared with £150 in the previous year. Sales will therefore decrease to $\dfrac{140}{150}$ of the previous year figure but increase by one-third in volume. Sales calculation is therefore

$$£180,000 \times \frac{140}{150} \times \frac{4}{3} = £224,000$$

WORKING 2

$$\frac{100}{140} \times £224,000 = £160,000$$

WORKING 3

	£
Cost of sales per Working (2)	160,000
less opening stock	31,000
	129,000
add closing stock	30,000
	£159,000

Question 22.3

Trading Account for the year ended 31 December 1981.

	£		£
Stock 1 January 1981	3,000	Sales	60,000
Purchases	47,000		
	50,000		
Stock 31 December 1981	4,500		
Cost of sales	45,500		
Gross profit	14,500		
	60,000		60,000

R. Sheldon presents you with the trading account set out above. He always calculates his selling price by adding $33\frac{1}{3}$ per cent of cost on to the cost price.

(a) If he had adhered strictly to the statement above, what should be the percentage of gross profit to sales?
(b) Calculate his actual percentage of gross profit to sales.
(c) Give two reasons for the difference between the figures you have calculated above.
(d) His suppliers are proposing to increase their prices by 5 per cent, but R. Sheldon considers that he would be unwise to increase his selling price. To obtain some impression of the effect on gross profit if his costs should be increased by 5 per cent, he asks you to reconstruct his trading account to show the gross profit if the increase had applied from 1 January 1981.
(e) Using the figures given in the trading account at the beginning of the question, calculate R. Sheldon's rate of stock turnover.

(f) R. Sheldon's expenses amount to 10 per cent of his sales. Calculate his net profit for the year ended 31 December 1981.

(g) If all expenses remained unchanged, but suppliers of stock increased their prices by 5 per cent as in (d) above, calculate the percentage reduction in the amount of net profit which R. Sheldon's accounts would have shown.

(L)

Answer 22.3

(a) $\dfrac{33\frac{1}{3}}{133\frac{1}{3}} \times 100 = 25$ per cent

(b) $\dfrac{14,500}{60,000} \times 100 = 24.17$ per cent

(c) (i) Selling prices reduced.
    (ii) Stock lost or stolen.

(d)

	£		£
Stock 1 January 1981	3,000	Sales	60 000
Purchases	49,350		
	52,350		
Stock 31 December 1983	4,725		
Cost of Sales	47,625		
Gross profit	12,375		
	60,000		60 000

(e) $\dfrac{£45,500 \text{ (cost of sales)}}{£3,750 \text{ (average stock)}} = 12.13$ times

or

$\dfrac{£45,500 \text{ (cost of sales)}}{£4,500 \text{ (closing stock)}} = 10.11$ times

(f)

	£
Gross profit	14,500
Expenses (10 per cent × £60,000)	6,000
Net profit	£8,500

(g) $\dfrac{(14,500 - 12,375)}{8,500} = 25.00$ per cent

23 Funds Flow Statements

23.1   Purpose of funds flow statements

So far, in the preparation of final accounts, we have concerned ourselves mainly with two statements: first, the profit and loss account, which tells us the profit or loss for the accounting period and how that profit or loss has been arrived at; second, the balance sheet, which provides us with details of assets and liabilities at that date.

There are, however, some important questions which may be asked about the accounts for the business which are not readily answered by the above two statements. Some of these questions will be:

(a) Why, if we have made a profit, hasn't the bank balance increased by the same amount?
(b) How is it that, although we have made a loss, the bank balance has not decreased by all that much?
(c) What has happened to all the money we received when we sold off some fixed assets?

In order to answer the above questions, we need to prepare a statement which reconciles the net profit to the change in bank balances. This statement we call a funds flow statement.

23.2   Preparation of the funds flow statement

From what we have stated above, we can deduce that we need the following items in our statement of reconciliation:

(a) net profit;
(b) funds from other sources, e.g. sale of fixed assets;
(c) change in cash or bank balances.

First, let us consider item (a) and its effect upon the change in bank balance. We might initially expect our bank balance to improve by the amount of our net profit. However, there will be some items of expenditure which do not mean cash has gone out of the business. The most common of these non-cash expenses is depreciation, since the fixed assets have been paid for in a previous accounting period. This means that our bank balance will improve to the extent of the net profit *before* any non-cash expenses are charged. The net profit figure to be used in our funds flow statement needs to be the net profit from our profit and loss account, with an adjustment to add back any non-cash expenses.

We shall now turn our attention to another important item in our funds flow statement, which is the increase or decrease in working capital items (e.g. stocks, debtors and creditors). To explain these working capital items, let us consider the following simple example.

On Saturday morning Alan, who runs a stall selling shirts in a street market, starts the day with 50 shirts, which cost him £10 each. His stock is therefore worth £500, and since he has no other assets or liabilities, this represents his capital. During the day he sells all of the shirts for £15 each, thus making a profit of £250 (50 x £5). On Monday morning he goes to his supplier and replaces the stock by purchasing 50 shirts at £12 each. Let us compare his balance sheet now with how it would have looked on Saturday morning.

	Before	Now
Assets		
Stock	500	600
Cash	–	150 (1)
	500	750
Capital	500	750 (2)

WORKINGS

    (1) Sales £750 less replacement of stock £600.

    (2) Opening capital of £500 plus profit of £250.

We can now reconcile his profit to his change in cash as follows:

Net profit	250
less increase in stock (£600 – £500)	100
Increase in cash balance	£150

We can see that the bank balance has not increased by the net profit made, because of an increase in stock.

If Alan were to sell on credit, a similar adjustment would be necessary in respect of an increase in debtors. That is to say, in reconciling net profit to change in cash or bank balance we must make a deduction for any increase in debtors.

Conversely, if Alan can negotiate credit terms with his suppliers, this will benefit his cash balance, since he has stock which he has not paid for. This will mean that in our reconciliation we must add to the net profit any increase in creditors.

You will probably have started to realise that the reconciliation can best be prepared by an examination of the two balance sheets, and this is a recommended approach. Changes in balance sheet figures will represent either an increase in cash balance, which we call a source of funds, or a reduction in cash balance, which we refer to as an application of funds.

We can now summarise all that we have looked at so far and categorise the adjustments into sources of funds and applications.

Source of funds	*Application of funds*
(1) Net profit (with any depreciation added back)	(1) Purchase of fixed assets
(2) Sale of fixed assets	(2) Any increase in current assets, such as debtors and stocks
(3) Any increase in liabilities, such as creditors	(3) Any decrease in liabilities, such as creditors
(4) Any decrease in current assets, such as debtors and stock	

The last item in each column has not been mentioned so far, except that they are the reverse effects of the events previously examined.

Just as an increase in stock and/or debtors will decrease our cash balance, so a reduction in those items will increase our cash balance. Similarly, in the same way that an increase in creditors helps our cash balance, so a decrease in creditors will have an adverse effect upon it.

You may find it a good idea to refer back constantly to the above table in looking at the worked examples and further exercises.

23.3 Worked examples

Example 23.1

The following Balance Sheets relate to a business run by Trevor Jordan:

	£ 31 Dec. 1985		£ 31 Dec. 1986	
Fixed Assets		40,000		70,000
Current Assets				
Stock	8,000		26,000	
Debtors	2,000		4,000	
Bank	22,000		2,000	
	32,000		32,000	
Creditors	4,000		12,000	
Working Capital		28,000		20,000
		68,000		90,000
Capital		68,000		80,000
Loan				10,000
		£68,000		£90,000

Trevor considers he has not done well, since his bank balance has decreased from £22,000 to £2,000 in spite of the fact that he has borrowed £10,000 and left £12,000 of his profit in the business.

(a) Set out a statement showing Trevor how the money has been spent.
(b) Comment on Trevor's judgement of his success.

Solution 23.1

(a)
Statement of source and application of funds for the year ended 31 December 1986

Source of funds		£
Net profit left in business (1)		12,000
Increase in creditors		8,000
Increase in loan		10,000
		30,000
Application of funds		
Increase in fixed assets	30,000	
Increase in stock	18,000	
Increase in debtors	2,000	
		50,000
(Decrease) in bank balance		£(20,000)

WORKING

(1) Calculated from change in capital balance (£80,000 less £68,000).

(b) The above statement demonstrates that funds generated by trading are increased by additional credit taken and loan raised. However, the purchase of fixed assets and increased levels of stocks and debtors amount to more than the sources of funds, which causes an overall decrease in the bank balance.

Example 23.2

The following Balance Sheets relate to the business of Martin Calaby.

		£ 31 Jan. 1986		£ 31 Jan. 1987
Fixed Assets				
Buildings		40,000		68,000
Fixtures	15,000		18,000	
less Depreciation	5,000	10,000	6,500	11,500
Motor vehicle	10,000		10,000	
less Depreciation	5,000	5,000	7,500	2,500
		55,000		82,000
Current Assets				
Stock	4,000		6,210	
Debtors	6,000		8,610	
Bank	1,600		–	
Cash	100		50	
	11,700		14,870	
less Current Liabilities				
Creditors	3,000		3,400	
Bank overdraft	–		6,700	
	3,000		10,000	
Working capital		8,700		4,770
		£63,700		£86,770
Capital at 1 February		61,860		63,700
add Cash introduced		–		20,000
add Net profit for year		17,800		21,070
		79,660		104,770
less Drawings		15,960		18,000
		£63,700		£ 86,770

Prepare a source and application of funds statement.

Solution 23.2

Statement of source and application of funds for the year ended 31 January 1987

	£
Source of funds	
Net profit for year	21,070
add back Depreciation (1)	4,000
Generated from trading operations	25,070
Increase in Creditors	400
Cash introduced	20,000
	45,470

201

Application of funds

Purchase of buildings	28,000	
Purchase of fixtures	3,000	
Increase in Stock	2,210	
Increase in Debtors	2,610	
Drawings	18,000	
		53,820

Net decrease in Cash and Bank balances (2)   £ 8,350

WORKINGS

(1) Increase in Depreciation provision

Fixtures (£6,500 – £5,000)	1,500
Motor vehicle (£7,500 – £5,000)	2,500
	4,000

(2) Change in Bank balance from £1,600 to overdraft of £6,700 represents a

Decrease of	£8,300
Decrease in Cash in hand	50
	£8,350

23.4   Further exercise

Question 23.1

John Drakes, a sole trader, has provided the following balance sheets:

Drakes – Balance Sheets as at 31 March

	1986 Cost £	1986 Dep'n £	1986 Net £	1987 Cost £	1987 Dep'n £	1987 Net £
Fixed Assets						
Freehold land	20,000		20,000	20,000		20,000
Fittings	1,000	750	250	1,200	870	330
Vehicle	800	400	400	800	600	200
	£21,800	£1,150	20,650	£22,000	£1,470	20,530
Current Assets						
Stock		11,000			15,400	
Debtors		1,000			540	
Cash		9,550			3,030	
		21,550			18,970	
Current Liabilities						
Creditors		12,000			8,000	
Net Current Assets			9,550			10,970
			£30,200			£31,500
representing:						
Capital brought forward			28,000			30,200
add:						
Profit for the year			5,400			5,800
			33,400			36,000

less:

Drawings	3,200	4,500
	£30,200	£31,500

You are required to prepare a statement of sources and application of funds for the year to 31 March 1987.

Answer 23.1

Statement of source and application of funds for the year ended 31 March 1987

Source of funds

Net profit		5,800
add back depreciation		320
Generated from trading operations		6,120
Decrease in Debtors		460
		6,580

Application of funds

Purchase of fittings	200	
Increase in Stock	4,400	
Decrease in Creditors	4,000	
Drawings	4,500	
		13,100
(Decrease) in Cash balance		£(6,520)

24 Multiple Choice Questions

24.1 Introduction

Many of the examining boards include in their papers a section with multiple choice questions. These questions do no more than test your knowledge of accounting within areas covered elsewhere in this book. However, just as with all types of questions in all examinations, familiarity with the style of question with which you will be faced is important.

24.2 Worked examples

Example 24.1

Given below are questions/statements followed by four possible answers, and you are required to select the correct or most appropriate answer.

1 The total of the Sales day book:
   A Is posted to the debit of the Sales account
   B Is posted to the credit of the Sales account
   C Is posted to the debit of the personal account of the business to whom the goods were sold
   D Is not posted to the ledger

2 Invoices received for goods purchased would first be entered in:
   A The Sales day book
   B The Purchases account
   C The Purchases day book
   D The cash book

3 The entries for Loan interest received are:
   A Debit bank account   Credit Loan account
   B Credit Bank account   Debit Loan account
   C Credit Bank account   Debit Loan Interest account
   D Debit Bank account   Credit Loan Interest account

4 Credit balances on accounts are:
   A Either liabilities or gains
   B Either assets or losses
   C Profits only
   D Losses only

5 If premises were let on January 1 at an annual rental of £100 and the amounts paid for the year ended June 30 totalled £75, the Profit and Loss account should show the rent as:
   A £75   B £50   C £100   D £125

6 Gross profit is:
   A Sales minus purchases
   B Net profit minus expenses
   C Sales minus cost of goods sold
   D None of these
7 The cost of goods sold is:
   A Purchases
   B Sales
   C Sales minus cost of sales
   D Stock at start plus purchases minus stock at end
8 A Balance Sheet is:
   A Part of the double entry
   B A ledger account
   C A statement of outstanding balances after the preparation of the Trading and Profit and Loss accounts
   D Prepared only to prove the arithmetical accuracy of the accounts
9 A provision for bad and doubtful debts is created:
   A To cancel a particular bad debt
   B To provide for possible bad debts
   C When a debtor becomes bankrupt
   D When debts are outstanding for over two months
10 The balance on the Provision for bad and doubtful debts account would:
   A Appear on the trial balance as a debit
   B Appear on the trial balance as a credit
   C Not appear on the trial balance
   D Be transferred to the personal account concerned
11 The balance of the Provision for depreciation account:
   A Is shown on the trial balance as a debit
   B Is shown on the trial balance as a credit
   C Is not shown on the trial balance, as it is included in Depreciation
   D Is not shown on the trial balance, as it has already been deducted from the asset concerned
12 Debentures are:
   A The same as Ordinary shares
   B The same as Preference shares
   C Certificates showing that loans have been made to the company
   D Shares which cannot be paid back to the shareholders
13 Which of these would appear as a current liability in the Balance Sheet:
   A Wages due
   B Rent receivable due
   C Insurance premium paid in advance
   D Advertising charges carried forward
14 In a trial balance Purchases:
   A Would be shown on the debit side
   B Would be shown on the credit side
   C Would not appear unless they were credit purchases only
   D Would not appear unless they were cash purchases only
15 A firm repays a loan to A. Paul of £6,000. The entries would be:
   A Debit Bank account   Credit Loan account
   B Debit Loan account   Credit Bank account
   C Credit Bank account   Debit Loan Interest account
   D Debit Bank account   Credit Loan Interest account

16 Which of the following accounts is a Personal account:
   A Premises
   B Depreciation
   C Sales
   D Wye Tool Co. Ltd
17 The owner of a business takes stock for his own use. The entries should be:
   A Debit Purchases   Credit Drawings
   B Debit Drawings   Credit Stock
   C Debit Drawings   Credit Purchases
   D Debit Stock   Credit Drawings
18 Mr T. Smith introduces a further £1,500 cash into his business. The entries should be:
   A Debit Capital   Credit Sales
   B Debit Cash   Credit Sales
   C Debit Cash only
   D Debit Cash   Credit Capital
19 A. Brewster, who runs a florist's shop, makes the following payments. Which of these is considered to be capital expenditure?
   A Purchase of 100 dozen daffodils
   B Payment of £100 wages
   C Purchase of a delivery van
   D Payment of £50 electricity bill
20 C. Williams, a baker, buys new fittings on credit for one of his shops. This transaction should first be entered in:
   A The cash book
   B The purchases day book
   C The ledger
   D The journal

Solution 24.1

1. **B**; 2. **C**; 3. **D**; 4. **A**; 5. **B**; 6. **C**; 7. **D**; 8. **C**; 9. **B**; 10. **B**; 11. **B**; 12. **C**; 13. **A**; 14.**A**; 15. **B**; 16. **D**; 17. **C**; 18. **D**; 19. **C**; 20. **D**

Example 24.2

Given below are questions/statements followed by three answers, and you are required to indicate which of them is correct. Only one, two or all three may be correct.

   1 Accounting is helpful to a business because it provides information:
      A Of past profits/losses
      B For estimating future results
      C For analysing labour turnover
   2 Which of the following may be used to make entries in the bank columns of the cash book?
      A Cheques received from debtors
      B Business standing orders
      C Copy sales invoices

3   Study the following account and then answer the question below.

Summarised Bank Account

	£		£
Debtors' payments	80,000	Balance b/d	4,000
Net profit	15,000	Expenses	10,000
		Purchases	50,000
		Depreciation	5,000
		Balance c/d	26,000
	95,000		95,000
Balance b/d	26,000		

Assuming the figures are arithmetically correct, which of the following should *not* have been entered in the account?
A   Depreciation
B   Net profit
C   Debtors' payments

4   Which of the following items may appear in a creditors' ledger control account?
A   Cash paid to suppliers
B   Purchase returns
C   Discounts received

5   Which of the following items would cause a trial balance to disagree?
A   Omission of a debtors' account
B   Overvaluation of closing stock
C   Failing to make a provision for bad debts

6   Dawn receives a bank statement which does not agree with her cash book balance. Which of the following may be responsible for this difference?
A   Cheques paid in have not been credited
B   The bank has charged overdraft interest
C   A cheque sent to a supplier has not been presented

7. Which of the following accounts in the ledger of a firm would have a credit balance?
A   Rent receivable account
B   Overdrawn bank account
C   Discount allowed account

8   Which of the following errors would affect the balancing of a trial balance?
A   An amount posted to A. Harris instead of B. Harris
B   An amount omitted entirely from the books
C   An amount posted to the wrong side of the account

9   It is usual, at the end of the financial year, to provide for depreciation of fixed assets. This is so that:
A   The cost of such assets will be written off over their useful life
B   The loss of value which some fixed assets suffer over a period of years will be accounted for
C   Cash will be provided to pay for new assets when replacement becomes necessary

10 At the end of a financial year a businessman would show rent he had paid in advance as:
A   An expense charged in the Profit and Loss account
B   A liability in the Balance Sheet
C   A debit balance carried down in the Rent account

1. **A** and **B**; 2. **A** and **B**; 3. **A** and **B**; 4. **A, B** and **C**; 5. **A**; 6. **A, B** and **C**; 7. **A** and **B**; 8. **C**; 9. **A** and **B**; 10. **C**

24.3   Further exercises

Question 24.1

Given below are questions/statements followed by four possible answers, and you are required to select the correct or most appropriate answer.

1   The owner of a travel business pays out £400 cash for wages for work done on extending his premises. The entries in the ledger should be:
   A   Credit Cash   Debit Wages
   B   Credit Cash   Debit Sundry expenses
   C   Credit Cash   Debit Premises account
   D   There is no need to enter this transaction, as it had nothing to do with a bakery business

2   Trade discount is shown in
   A   The sales or purchases day book only
   B   The sales or purchases day book and the ledger
   C   The cash book only
   D   The cash book and the ledger

3   D. Smithers's account in a business's ledger shows a debit balance of £200 on 1 January. During the month the business sold goods to D. Smithers invoiced at £250 less 20 per cent trade discount, and received a cheque from D. Smithers for £156 on account after a cash discount of 2.5 per cent had been deducted. The balance on the account at the end of the month would be
   A   £240 debit
   B   £244 debit
   C   £290 debit
   D   £290 credit

4   The trial balance showed wages £2,500 and a note stated that £500 wages were due but unpaid. When preparing final accounts you should:
   A   Debit Profit and Loss account £3,000 and show Wages accrued £500 in the Balance Sheet
   B   Debit Profit and Loss account £2,000 and show Wages accrued £500 in the Balance Sheet
   C   Debit Profit and Loss account £3,000 and show Wages prepaid £500 in the Balance Sheet
   D   Debit Profit and Loss account £2,000 and show Wages paid in advance £500

5   Carriage outwards is shown on the:
   A   Debit of Profit and Loss account
   B   Credit of Profit and Loss account
   C   Debit of Trading account
   D   Credit of Trading account

6   If after preparing a balance sheet a cheque for £30 was paid to a creditor, the alterations to the balance sheet would be:
   A   Increase Debtors £40, decrease Creditors £40
   B   Decrease Bank account by £40 only
   C   Decrease Bank account by £40, decrease Creditors by £40
   D   Only decrease Creditors by £40

7 Liquid assets are:

    A The difference between Fixed Assets and Current Assets

    B Cash and anything that can be turned into cash quickly

    C Cash only

    D The difference between Current Assets and Current Liabilities

8 The balance on the sales ledger control account in the general ledger is usually:

    A A credit balance

    B A debit balance

    C Either **A** or **B**

    D None: it should balance itself like a trial balance

9 A business purchased goods from S. W. Weston Ltd for £56. In error this was posted to the debit of S. W. Weston Ltd account. The entries to correct this error are:

    A Credit S. W. Weston Ltd £56   Debit suspense account £56

    B Credit S. W. Weston Ltd £112   Debit suspense account £112

    C Credit Purchases account £56   Debit suspense account £56

    D Credit Purchases account £112 only

10 The bank statement shows a credit balance of £135. When preparing a bank reconciliation statement, it is found that cheques drawn but not yet presented for payment amounted to £263 and that there was a standing order for £7, in the bank statement but not in the cash book. What was the original balance in the cash book?

    A £121 credit

    B £128 credit

    C £405 debit

    D £391 credit

11 P. Peters, who owes £100, is bankrupt and a first and final dividend of 25p in the pound is received. The entries to record this should be:

    A Debit Bank account £25   Credit P. Peters account £25

        Debit Bad Debts account £75   Credit P. Peters account £75

    B Credit P. Peters account £100   Debit Bad Debts account £100

    C Debit Bank £75   Credit P. Peters account £75

        Debit Bad Debts account £25   Credit P. Peters account £25

    D Debit Bank account £100   Credit P. Peters account £100

12 A trial balance shows Provision for Bad Debts £190 and Debtors £6,800. It is required to write off a further £320 as bad debts and maintain the provision at 2.5 per cent of debtors. To do this the profit and loss should show:

    A A credit of £20 and a debit of £320

    B A credit of £28 and a debit of £320

    C A credit of £490

    D A credit of £394

13 Which of the following is not a method of depreciation?

    A Fixed instalment

    B Reducing balance

    C Straight line

    D Revaluation

    E None: they are all methods of depreciation

14 The Plant and Machinery account has a balance of £45,000 and the Provision for Depreciation account a balance of £22,000. A machine which was bought two years previously for £14,000 was sold for £5,000. The plant and machinery has been depreciated at 20 per cent on cost. The balance on the provision for depreciation after this sale was:

    A £22,000

    B £16,000

C £16,400

D £400

15 The Receipts and Payments account shows:

   A The actual cash receipts and payments made during the period

   B What the receipts and payments should have been during the period

   C The accumulated fund

   D The profit and loss for the period

16 The difference between direct and indirect expenses is:

   A Direct expenses are a prime cost but indirect expenses are factory over-heads

   B Direct expenses are factory overheads but indirect expenses are a prime cost

   C Direct expenses vary directly with wages but indirect expenses have no relation to wages

   D Direct expenses are directly concerned with production but indirect expenses are only partly concerned with production

17 If there is no partnership deed, then profits and losses:

   A Can be divided just as the partners wish

   B Must be shared equally

   C Must be shared in the same proportion as capitals

   D Must be shared equally, after an adjustment for interest on capital has been made

18 In a partnership where capitals are fixed, an item in the Appropriation account shows partners' salaries £2,100. The double entry for this would be:

   A Debit Profit and Loss account

   B Credit Capital account

   C Debit Current account

   D Credit Current account

19 To create a provision for discounts allowed, the necessary entries would be:

   A Debit Profit and Loss account Credit Provision for Discounts account

   B Credit Profit and Loss account Debit Provision for Discounts account

   C Debit Customers' accounts Credit Provision for Discounts account

   D Debit Discount Allowed account Credit Provision for Discounts account

20 Which of the following transactions would affect the capital of a business?

   A Goods for resale purchased on credit

   B A receipt from a debtor of £210

   C A sale of goods which cost £150 on credit for £220

   D A purchase of a machine for £350

Answer 24.1

1. C; 2. A; 3. A; 4. A; 5. A; 6. C; 7. B; 8. B; 9. B; 10. A; 11. A; 12. A; 13. E; 14. C; 15. A; 16. A; 17. B; 18. D; 19. A; 20. C

Question 24.2

Given below are questions/statements followed by three answers and you are required to indicate which of them is correct. One, two or all three may be correct.

1 In the final accounts of a business, carriage inwards should be included in the:

   A Trading account

   B Profit and Loss account

   C Appropriation account

2   The annual profit of a firm is not an exact figure, but an estimate calculated from the accounting information available. Which of the following items is/are only an estimated charge?
    A   Depreciation of fixed assets
    B   Provision for doubtful debts
    C   Cash paid in advance for expenses
3   In a partnership, which of the following would appear in the appropriation account?
    A   Interest on capital
    B   Interest on drawings
    C   Interest on bank overdraft
4   Which of the following items should be taken into account by a firm when calculating its credit sales?
    A   Opening debtors
    B   Closing debtors
    C   Discount received
5   A debenture holder in a limited liability company is:
    A   Paid a fixed rate of interest each year
    B   A creditor of the company
    C   A part owner of the assets of the company
6   Which of the following should be included in the appropriation account of a limited liability company?
    A   Dividend paid to shareholders
    B   Sum transferred to general reserve
    C   Interest paid to debenture holders
7   Which of the following provisions in the Partnership Act, 1890, apply where no agreement exists?
    A   Profits and losses must be shared equally
    B   Interest shall be paid on drawings
    C   Interest on capital shall be paid at 5 per cent per annum
8   Which of the following correctly define the authorised capital of a limited liability company?
    A   Capital registered with the Registrar of Joint Stock Companies
    B   Capital issued by the managing directors
    C   Capital subscribed by the directors
9   Which of the following items should be used in the calculation of purchases to be charged to the trading account for a firm not keeping proper books of account?
    A   Cash received from trade debtors
    B   Goods at cost price taken by the proprietor for his own use
    C   Discounts received from trade creditors
10 Which of the following measures the profitability of a business?
    A   The total of the trade debtors
    B   Amount of cash at the bank
    C   Return on capital employed

Answer 24.2

1. **A**; 2. **A** and **B**; 3. **A** and **B**; 4. **A** and **B**; 5. **A** and **B**; 6. **A** and **B**; 7. **A**; 8. **A**; 9. **B** and **C**; 10. **C**

Index